I0007402

Web Development with Rails 8 and PostgreSQL: A Practical Beginner's Course

Matt P. Handy

Copyright © 2025 Matt P. Handy

All rights reserved.

No part of this book may be reproduced, stored in a retrieval system, or transmitted in any form or by any means, electronic, mechanical, photocopying, recording, or otherwise, without the prior written permission of the copyright owner.

Table of Contents

Introduction

Welcome to the world of web development! If you're holding this book, chances are you're curious about building websites and web applications. Maybe you've got a brilliant idea for an online business, want to create a personal blog, or simply want to learn a valuable new skill. Whatever your reason, you've come to the right place.

This book is designed to be your friendly guide to learning web development using two powerful and popular technologies: **Rails 8** and **PostgreSQL**.

• Target Audience and Prerequisites

Let's be clear about who this book is for. Are you an absolute beginner to programming? Don't worry! You don't need to be a computer whiz or have years of coding experience to get started. If you know how to use a computer, browse the internet, and are willing to learn, you've got everything you need.

However, to make the most of this book, it helps to have:

- **Basic Computer Skills:** Knowing how to use your operating system (Windows, macOS, or Linux), navigate files and folders, and use a web browser.
- **A Desire to Learn:** Web development can be challenging at times, but with patience and perseverance, you'll be surprised at how much you can accomplish.

We're not assuming you know anything about Ruby, Rails, or PostgreSQL. We'll start from the very beginning and guide you step-by-step.

• Why Rails 8 and PostgreSQL?

You might be wondering, "Why Rails and PostgreSQL? There are so many other technologies out there!" That's a fair question. Here's why we've chosen these tools for this course:

- **Rails is a Framework:** Rails is a web application framework written in the Ruby programming language. Think of it as a pre-built foundation for building websites. It provides a structure, tools, and conventions that make development faster, easier, and more organized.

- **Productivity:** Rails is known for its "convention over configuration" approach, which means that it makes intelligent assumptions about how you want to build your application. This reduces the amount of code you have to write and allows you to focus on the unique features of your project.
- **A Thriving Community:** Rails has a large and active community of developers who are always willing to help beginners. You'll find tons of online resources, tutorials, and forums where you can get support and connect with other learners.
- **PostgreSQL is a Robust Database:** PostgreSQL is a powerful, open-source relational database system. It's known for its reliability, scalability, and adherence to standards.
- **The Perfect Pair:** Rails and PostgreSQL work exceptionally well together. Rails has excellent support for PostgreSQL, making it easy to store and retrieve data.
- **My Personal Experience:** I've been working with Rails and PostgreSQL for over [insert number] years, and I can honestly say that it's a fantastic combination for building web applications. I've used it to create everything from small personal projects to large-scale enterprise systems. The productivity gains and the stability of the platform are simply unmatched.

• **Book Overview and Learning Goals**

This book is designed to be a **practical, hands-on course**. You won't just be reading about web development concepts; you'll be building real-world applications.

Here's a quick overview of what you'll learn:

- **Setting up your development environment:** We'll walk you through the process of installing Ruby, Rails, and PostgreSQL on your computer.
- **Understanding the fundamentals of Ruby:** We'll cover the essential Ruby concepts you need to know to work with Rails.
- **Building your first Rails application:** We'll guide you through the process of creating a simple "Hello, World" application.
- **Mastering the Model-View-Controller (MVC) architecture:** We'll explain how Rails uses MVC to organize your code.

- **Working with databases:** You'll learn how to create models, define database relationships, and perform CRUD (Create, Read, Update, Delete) operations.
- **Creating dynamic web pages:** You'll learn how to use views and templates to display data in your application.
- **Handling user input:** You'll learn how to create forms, validate user input, and process data.
- **Implementing user authentication and authorization:** You'll learn how to secure your application by adding user accounts and controlling access to resources.
- **Testing your application:** You'll learn how to write tests to ensure that your code is working correctly.
- **Deploying your application:** You'll learn how to deploy your application to a web server so that others can access it.

By the end of this book, you'll have the knowledge and skills to build your own web applications using Rails and PostgreSQL.

• **How to Use This Book Effectively**

To get the most out of this book, I recommend the following:

- **Follow Along:** Don't just read the code examples; type them into your computer and run them. Experiment with the code and see what happens when you change things.
- **Practice Regularly:** Web development is a skill that requires practice. The more you code, the better you'll become.
- **Don't Be Afraid to Ask for Help:** If you get stuck, don't hesitate to ask for help. There are plenty of online resources and communities where you can get support.
- **Stay Curious:** Web development is a constantly evolving field. Keep learning and exploring new technologies.
- **Take Breaks:** Staring at code for hours on end can be exhausting. Take breaks to clear your head and recharge.
- **Engage in the exercises**: At the end of each section, ensure you do the exercises at the end. This will make it easier for you to understand

This book is more than just a set of instructions; it's a guide to a fulfilling and rewarding career. Embrace the challenge, have fun, and let's build something amazing together!

Now, let's dive into the exciting world of web development with Rails and PostgreSQL!

Chapter 1: Web Development Fundamentals

Alright, let's kick things off with a foundational understanding of how the web works. Think of this chapter as your "Web Development 101" class. We'll break down the key concepts, and by the end, you'll have a solid grasp of the building blocks of the internet.

1.1 The Internet and Web Applications Explained: Your Digital Playground

The Internet, at its core, is a global network of interconnected computers. Think of it not just as a single entity, but a vast, sprawling web. These computers, located all over the world, are wired (or wirelessly) together, capable of communicating and exchanging data. This exchange isn't random; it follows specific rules, or *protocols*, that ensure everyone speaks the same language. This is the foundation of what allows you to read this text, watch videos, and connect with people globally.

But we're not just passively receiving data, right? We're interacting. This brings us to *web applications*.

What Makes a Web Application a "Web Application"?

A web application is simply software that you access via a web browser – your Chrome, Firefox, Safari, or Edge. Critically, it's distinct from software installed directly on your computer (a "desktop application"). Instead of living on your hard drive, web applications exist (mostly) on a server and you "visit" them through your browser.

Think of a few examples you likely use every day:

- **Social Media:** Platforms like Twitter/X, Instagram, and Facebook are sophisticated web applications that let you connect, share, and consume content.
- **E-commerce:** Online stores such as Amazon and eBay let you browse, purchase, and manage your orders, all within your browser.
- **Cloud-based Productivity:** Services like Google Docs and Microsoft 365 allow you to create and edit documents, spreadsheets, and presentations, all stored and accessed online.

- **Banking:** Your bank's website or mobile app (which is often a web app wrapped in a native container) lets you manage your accounts, transfer funds, and pay bills.

Why Web Applications Are So Powerful

The beauty of web applications lies in their accessibility and portability. Because they run in a browser, you can access them from virtually any device with an internet connection, regardless of the operating system. This ease of access is a significant advantage.

Moreover, updates and maintenance are centralized. Instead of pushing updates to individual users' computers, the developers simply update the server-side code, and everyone benefits immediately.

The Difference Between a Website and a Web Application

This is a common point of confusion. While the terms are often used interchangeably, there's a subtle but important distinction.

- **Website:** Generally static, primarily designed to display information. Think of a brochure or online magazine.
- **Web Application:** Highly interactive, designed to allow users to *do* things – create content, process transactions, manage data, etc. It is usually backed by a database, and involves complex server-side logic.

My Perspective: Early in my career, I built static websites. They were informative but passive. The shift to web applications felt like unlocking a new level of potential. Suddenly, I could create dynamic experiences, empowering users to participate and interact with the online world in meaningful ways.

Code Examples (Coming Up!)

Later in this book, we'll build a real-world web application using Rails 8 and PostgreSQL. You'll see firsthand how to create dynamic content, handle user input, and interact with a database. I'll show you, step-by-step, how to translate these concepts into working code.

Moving Forward

Understanding the internet and web applications is the first step in your journey to becoming a web developer. The next section will delve deeper into the different sides of web development—client-side and server-side—and how they work together to create the experiences we use every day. We're building a foundation, so take your time, absorb the information, and get ready to dive deeper!

1.2 Client-Side vs. Server-Side Development: The Two Halves of a Web App

Think of a web application as a play. You have the actors on stage – what you see and interact with. Then you have the stagehands, the lighting crew, the costume designers, and everyone working behind the scenes to make the show happen. Web development is similar; it's divided into two main realms: *client-side* and *server-side*. Understanding the distinction is crucial for navigating the web development landscape.

Client-Side: What the User Sees and Touches (Front-End)

The *client-side* is everything that happens in the user's web browser. It's the part of the application that users directly interact with. This is often called the "front-end." The primary technologies involved are:

- **HTML (HyperText Markup Language):** HTML provides the structure and content of a web page. It's like the blueprint of a building, defining where the text, images, videos, and other elements are placed.
- **CSS (Cascading Style Sheets):** CSS controls the visual styling of the page. It dictates the colors, fonts, layout, and overall appearance of the content defined by HTML. CSS is like the interior design of a building, determining the aesthetic.
- **JavaScript:** JavaScript adds interactivity and dynamic behavior. It allows you to create animations, handle user input, validate forms, and even make requests to the server without reloading the page (a concept known as AJAX). JavaScript is like the electrical system of a building, making things respond to your actions.

Example: When you click a button on a website, see a dropdown menu appear, or watch a loading animation, that's JavaScript at work. The layout and colors of that button, are CSS. The placement and the text of that button, is HTML.

Server-Side: The Engine Room (Back-End)

The *server-side* is everything that happens on the server. It's the part of the application that handles data storage, user authentication, business logic, and other backend tasks. This is often called the "back-end." The key components include:

- **Programming Languages:** Languages like Ruby (which we'll be using with Rails), Python, Java, PHP, Node.js, and others, provide the logic and instructions for the server to execute.
- **Web Frameworks:** Frameworks like Rails, Django, Spring, Laravel, and Express.js provide a structure and set of tools to simplify server-side development.
- **Databases:** Databases like PostgreSQL (which we'll be using), MySQL, MongoDB, and others, store and manage the application's data.

Example: When you log into a website, the server verifies your credentials against a database. When you place an order on an e-commerce site, the server processes your payment, updates inventory, and sends you a confirmation email. These are all server-side operations.

The Relationship: How They Work Together

Client-side and server-side development aren't independent; they work together in a coordinated dance. Here's how it typically works:

1. **The Client Makes a Request:** A user interacts with the client-side (e.g., clicks a button).
2. **The Client Sends a Request to the Server:** The client-side code sends a request to the server, asking for specific data or to perform a certain action.
3. **The Server Processes the Request:** The server-side code receives the request, processes it (possibly interacting with a database), and generates a response.
4. **The Server Sends a Response to the Client:** The server sends a response back to the client.
5. **The Client Renders the Response:** The client-side code receives the response and updates the user interface accordingly.

Analogy Time: Think of ordering a pizza online. Your browser shows you the menu, that's Client-Side. When you click to place an order, a signal is sent to the pizza restaurant (Server-Side) where they process your order, update the list of orders, and tell you it has been placed.

My Personal Experience: When I first started, I focused primarily on the front-end. It was exciting to create visually appealing and interactive interfaces. However, I quickly realized that the front-end was only half the story. The real power came from understanding how the back-end worked and how to connect the two sides together.

Practical Examples (Coming Soon):

In later chapters, as we build our Rails 8 and PostgreSQL application, you'll see exactly how these technologies interact. You'll write client-side code to display data from the database, handle user input, and communicate with the server. You'll also write server-side code to process requests, interact with the database, and send responses back to the client.

Key Takeaway: Understanding client-side and server-side development is essential for any web developer. It allows you to build complete, functional web applications that provide a seamless user experience. We will start with the back end and then move to the front. Now, get ready to dive deeper into Rails and PostgreSQL!

1.3 Introduction to Rails: Your Fast Track to Web Development

You've learned about the internet, web applications, and the distinction between client-side and server-side. Now it's time to introduce a key player in the world of web development: **Rails**.

Rails, often called "Ruby on Rails," is a powerful and popular *web application framework* written in the Ruby programming language. But what does that *actually* mean?

Think of Rails as a pre-packaged set of tools and guidelines designed to simplify and accelerate the process of building web applications. It provides a structure, a set of conventions, and a wealth of pre-built components that can save you countless hours of coding.

Instead of building every aspect of your application from scratch, you can leverage Rails' built-in functionality to handle common tasks like routing, database interaction, user authentication, and more. It allows you to focus on the unique features of *your* application, rather than reinventing the wheel.

Why Use a Framework Like Rails?

You might be asking, "Why not just write everything from scratch using Ruby?" While that's certainly possible, it's like building a house without a blueprint, power tools, or pre-fabricated materials. You *could* do it, but it would be a much longer, more complicated, and error-prone process.

Here are the key benefits of using Rails:

- **Convention Over Configuration:** This is a cornerstone of Rails philosophy. Rails makes intelligent assumptions about how you want to structure your application, reducing the amount of configuration you need to write. It's like having a skilled carpenter who understands your needs and automatically sets up the tools and materials for you. It doesn't remove configuration, but instead provides sensible defaults that you can override only when necessary.
- **Don't Repeat Yourself (DRY):** Rails promotes the DRY principle, which means avoiding code duplication. By writing reusable code components, you reduce the risk of errors and make your application easier to maintain. Rails offers many helper methods that simplify common coding tasks.
- **Rapid Development:** Rails is designed for speed. Its built-in generators, scaffolding, and conventions allow you to create basic application features in minutes, rather than hours or days. This rapid development cycle makes it ideal for prototyping, experimenting, and quickly bringing your ideas to life.
- **MVC Architecture:** Rails enforces the Model-View-Controller (MVC) architectural pattern, which separates the application's data (Model), user interface (View), and logic (Controller) into distinct components. This separation makes the application easier to organize, test, and maintain. We'll dive into MVC in detail in Chapter 5.
- **A Thriving Community:** The Rails community is vast, active, and incredibly supportive. You'll find a wealth of online resources, tutorials, libraries (called "gems" in the Ruby world), and forums where you can get help, share your knowledge, and connect with other Rails developers. This community support is invaluable, especially when you're just starting out.

- **Security Focus:** Rails has built-in security features and follows secure coding practices to protect your application from common vulnerabilities like SQL injection, cross-site scripting (XSS), and cross-site request forgery (CSRF).

What You Can Build with Rails

The possibilities are virtually endless. Rails has been used to build a wide range of web applications, from simple blogs and e-commerce sites to complex social networks and enterprise-level platforms. Here are just a few examples:

- **E-commerce:** Shopify, a popular platform for building online stores, is built on Rails.
- **Project Management:** Basecamp, a leading project management tool, is also a Rails application.
- **Social Networking:** Twitter started as a Rails application.
- **Streaming services:** Hulu built its services on top of Rails.

My Personal Experience: I remember the first time I used Rails, I was amazed at how quickly I could create a functional web application. Coming from a background of writing everything from scratch, Rails felt like a superpower. It allowed me to focus on the *ideas* behind the application, rather than getting bogged down in the nitty-gritty details of implementation.

Practical Implementation (Coming Soon!)

In the upcoming chapters, we'll put these benefits into action. You'll create your own Rails application from scratch, and you'll see firsthand how Rails simplifies and accelerates the development process. You'll learn how to use Rails' generators, build models and controllers, create views, and interact with the database.

Rails 8 and Beyond:

Rails continues to evolve, incorporating new features and improvements with each release. In later chapters, we'll explore how Rails 8 enhances existing capabilities, streamlines workflows, and boosts developer productivity.

Takeaway: Rails empowers you to build complex web applications faster, more efficiently, and with greater confidence. It's a tool that can truly unlock your potential as a web developer. So, get ready to embrace the Rails way and build something amazing!

1.4 Introduction to PostgreSQL: Your Reliable Data Store

You now know how Rails helps structure and manage the logic of your web applications. But where do you store all the *data* that powers those applications – the user accounts, the product details, the blog posts, and everything else? That's where **PostgreSQL** comes in.

PostgreSQL (often pronounced "post-gress-Q-L," or simply "Postgres") is a powerful, open-source *relational database management system (RDBMS)*. Think of it as a robust and reliable digital filing cabinet, designed to store, organize, and retrieve data efficiently and securely.

Unlike simple file storage, PostgreSQL provides a structured way to organize your data into tables, with relationships between those tables. This structured approach makes it easier to query, analyze, and manage large amounts of data.

Why Choose PostgreSQL?

There are many database systems available. So why are we focusing on PostgreSQL? Here's why it's an excellent choice, especially for Rails applications:

- **Open Source and Free:** PostgreSQL is completely open source, which means you can use it without paying any licensing fees. This makes it a cost-effective solution, especially for beginners and small projects.
- **Standards-Compliant:** Postgresql conforms with ANSI standards to reduce vendor lock-in.
- **Rock-Solid Reliability:** PostgreSQL is renowned for its stability and reliability. It's been around for decades and has a proven track record of handling demanding workloads in mission-critical applications. You can trust it to keep your data safe and accessible.
- **Data Integrity:** PostgreSQL places a strong emphasis on data integrity. It provides features like transactions, constraints, and foreign keys to ensure that your data remains accurate and consistent, even in the face of errors or failures.

- **Scalability:** PostgreSQL can scale to handle large amounts of data and high traffic loads. It supports features like partitioning, replication, and connection pooling to optimize performance and ensure availability.
- **Extensibility:** PostgreSQL is highly extensible, meaning you can add new features and functionality using extensions. There are extensions for everything from geographic data processing to full-text search.
- **Excellent Rails Integration:** Rails has excellent support for PostgreSQL. The Rails framework provides seamless integration with PostgreSQL, making it easy to connect to the database, create tables, query data, and perform other database operations.
- **Advanced Features:** PostgreSQL offers a wide range of advanced features, including support for JSON data, full-text search, geographic data, and more. These features can be invaluable for building complex and sophisticated web applications.

Key Concepts in PostgreSQL

Before we dive into practical examples, let's define a few key concepts:

- **Database:** A container for all your data. You typically have one database per application.
- **Table:** A collection of related data organized into rows and columns. Think of a spreadsheet, where each row represents a record and each column represents a field.
- **Row (Record):** A single entry in a table.
- **Column (Field):** A specific attribute or piece of information in a table.
- **SQL (Structured Query Language):** The standard language for interacting with relational databases. You use SQL to create tables, insert data, query data, update data, and delete data.

My Personal Experience: I've worked with several different database systems over the years, and I've always been impressed by PostgreSQL's robustness, flexibility, and adherence to standards. It's a database that I can rely on to handle whatever challenges I throw at it. The transition from other databases to PostgreSQL with Rails was incredibly smooth, highlighting the excellent integration between the two technologies.

Practical Examples (Coming Up!)

In later chapters, you'll learn how to connect your Rails application to a PostgreSQL database, create tables using migrations, insert data, query data, and perform other database operations. You'll see firsthand how easy it is to work with PostgreSQL in a Rails environment.

You'll also see the power of SQL in action, learning how to write queries to retrieve specific data, filter data, and join data from multiple tables.

The Takeaway:

PostgreSQL is a powerful and versatile database system that is well-suited for web applications built with Rails. Its reliability, data integrity features, scalability, and excellent Rails integration make it an excellent choice for beginners and experienced developers alike. So, get ready to explore the world of databases with PostgreSQL!

1.5 A First Look: The Request-Response Cycle - The Heartbeat of the Web

You've learned about the building blocks of web applications – the client-side, the server-side, Rails, and PostgreSQL. But how do all these pieces interact? The answer lies in the **Request-Response Cycle**. This cycle is the fundamental communication loop that powers virtually every interaction you have on the web. Understanding it is crucial to grasping how web applications function.

Think of it like a conversation: you ask a question (the request), and someone answers (the response). It's a simple concept, but it's the foundation of how information is exchanged on the internet.

Breaking Down the Cycle

Let's break down the Request-Response Cycle into its core steps:

1. **The Client Initiates a Request:** This is where *you* come in, the user. You might type a URL into your browser's address bar, click a link, submit a form, or perform some other action that triggers a request. The client, in this case, is your web browser (Chrome, Firefox, Safari, etc.). The request is essentially a message sent from your

browser to a web server, asking for a specific resource. This resource could be an HTML page, an image, a video, or some other data.

2. **The Request Travels to the Server:** The request travels across the internet to the web server that hosts the website or application you're trying to access. The server is a powerful computer that's constantly listening for incoming requests.

3. **The Server Processes the Request:** Once the server receives the request, it needs to figure out what to do with it. This is where the server-side code (often powered by Rails, in our case) comes into play. The server may need to:
   o Retrieve data from a database (using PostgreSQL).
   o Perform calculations or business logic.
   o Generate an HTML page.
   o Authenticate a user.
   o Perform some other action.

4. **The Server Constructs a Response:** After processing the request, the server prepares a response. The response is a message that contains the data or information that the client requested. The response typically includes:
   o **An HTTP Status Code:** A numeric code that indicates whether the request was successful (e.g., 200 OK) or if there was an error (e.g., 404 Not Found, 500 Internal Server Error).
   o **Headers:** Metadata about the response, such as the content type (e.g., text/html, image/jpeg) and the length of the content.
   o **The Body:** The actual data that the client requested. This could be an HTML document, an image file, a JSON payload, or some other type of data.

5. **The Server Sends the Response:** The server sends the response back to the client.

6. **The Client Receives and Renders the Response:** Your browser receives the response and interprets it. If the response contains HTML, the browser renders the HTML to display a web page. If the response contains an image, the browser displays the image. If the response contains JSON data, the browser's JavaScript code can use the data to update the page dynamically.

Simplified Analogy

Imagine you're ordering coffee at a coffee shop:

1. **You (the Client) place your order (the Request) with the barista.**

2. **The barista (the Server) receives your order.**
3. **The barista prepares your coffee (processes the request, potentially accessing ingredients – the database).**
4. **The barista hands you your coffee (the Response).**
5. **You (the Client) enjoy your coffee (render the response).**

My Personal "Aha!" Moment

I remember struggling with web development until I truly grasped the Request-Response Cycle. Once I understood how the client and server communicated, everything else started to fall into place. It's a fundamental concept that unlocks a deeper understanding of how the web works.

The Role of Rails and PostgreSQL

Rails simplifies the process of handling requests and generating responses on the server-side. It provides a structure for organizing your code, handling routing, interacting with the database (PostgreSQL), and rendering views. PostgreSQL is responsible for storing and retrieving the data that the server needs to process requests and generate responses.

Practical Implementation (Coming Soon!)

In later chapters, you'll see the Request-Response Cycle in action as we build our Rails application. You'll write code to handle incoming requests, interact with the database, and generate responses that are displayed in the browser. You'll also learn how to use the Rails console to inspect requests and responses.

Key Takeaway:

The Request-Response Cycle is the heartbeat of the web. It's the fundamental communication loop that enables all the interactions you have with web applications. By understanding this cycle, you'll gain a deeper appreciation for how the web works and how you can build your own web applications using Rails and PostgreSQL. This understanding is critical to the code you will write from this point forward.

Chapter 2: Setting Up Your Development Environment - Your Web Dev Workshop

Welcome to the "construction zone"! Before we can start building amazing web applications, we need to set up our development environment. Think of this as setting up your workshop – you need the right tools and a comfortable workspace to get the job done. Don't worry, I'll walk you through each step, and we'll make it as painless as possible.

A good development environment is crucial. It's where you'll write code, run tests, and see your creations come to life. A well-configured environment can significantly boost your productivity and make the development process more enjoyable.

2.1 Installing Ruby: Your Foundation for Rails

Before you can build anything with Rails, you need to install Ruby, the language that powers the framework. While it might seem tempting to just download and install Ruby directly, that can lead to headaches down the road. That's why we'll be using *version managers*. Think of them as specialized toolboxes that let you easily switch between different versions of Ruby as needed.

Why is this important? Sometimes, older projects require older versions of Ruby to function correctly. A version manager allows you to maintain multiple Ruby versions on your system simultaneously, avoiding conflicts and ensuring that each project uses the correct Ruby version.

We'll focus on two popular version managers: rbenv and asdf. rbenv is laser-focused on managing Ruby versions, making it relatively simple to use. asdf, on the other hand, is a more versatile tool that can manage versions of many different languages, including Ruby, Node.js, Python, and more.

Choosing the Right Tool:

- **rbenv:** If you primarily work with Ruby and want a straightforward, easy-to-learn version manager, rbenv is an excellent choice. It's less complex to configure, especially for beginners.

- **asdf:** If you work with multiple languages and want a single tool to manage all your language versions, asdf is a great option. It has a steeper learning curve, but its versatility can be beneficial in the long run.

I'll provide instructions for both rbenv and asdf so you can choose the one that best suits your needs.

Option 1: Installing Ruby with rbenv

rbenv is a lightweight and powerful Ruby version manager. It allows you to install and switch between different Ruby versions easily. Here's how to install it:

macOS (using Homebrew):

1. **Install Homebrew (if you haven't already):** This is a package manager for macOS that simplifies the installation of software. Open your terminal and run:

   ```
   /bin/bash -c "$(curl -fsSL
   https://raw.githubusercontent.com/Homebrew/install/HEAD/install.sh)"
   ```

2. **Install rbenv:**

   ```
   brew install rbenv
   ```

3. **Configure your shell:** To make rbenv work correctly, you need to add it to your shell's configuration file (either ~/.zshrc for Zsh or ~/.bashrc for Bash). Add the following lines to the end of the file:

   ```
   eval "$(rbenv init -)"
   ```

   You can use a text editor like nano or vim to edit the file. For example, to edit ~/.zshrc with nano, run:

   ```
   nano ~/.zshrc
   ```

Paste the lines at the end of the file, save it (Ctrl+O in nano), and exit (Ctrl+X in nano).

4. **Restart your terminal or source your shell configuration file:** To apply the changes, either close and reopen your terminal or run:

```
source ~/.zshrc   # If you're using Zsh
source ~/.bashrc  # If you're using Bash
```

5. **Install a Ruby version:** To install a specific Ruby version (e.g., 3.2.2), run:

```
rbenv install 3.2.2
```

You can list available Ruby versions by running rbenv install -l.

6. **Set the global Ruby version:** To set the default Ruby version for all your projects, run:

```
rbenv global 3.2.2
```

7. **Verify the installation:** To confirm that Ruby is installed correctly, run:

```
ruby -v
```

Linux (using apt - Debian/Ubuntu): Adapt these instructions for your specific distribution and package manager.

1. **Install Dependencies:**

```
sudo apt update
sudo apt install git curl build-essential libssl-dev
libreadline-dev zlib1g-dev
```

2. **Clone rbenv repository:**

```
git clone https://github.com/rbenv/rbenv.git ~/.rbenv
```

3. **Configure your shell:** Add rbenv to your path and enable initialization:

```
echo 'export PATH="$HOME/.rbenv/bin:$PATH"' >>
~/.bashrc
echo 'eval "$(rbenv init -)"' >> ~/.bashrc
```

4. **Source your shell:**

```
source ~/.bashrc
```

5. **Install ruby-build plugin:** This plugin allows you to easily install different Ruby versions.

```
git clone https://github.com/rbenv/ruby-build.git
~/.rbenv/plugins/ruby-build
```

6. **Install Ruby and set global version:** (Same as steps 5 and 6 above for macOS)
7. **Verify:** (Same as macOS step 7)

Windows (using WSL - Windows Subsystem for Linux):

Follow the Linux instructions above within your WSL terminal.

Option 2: Installing Ruby with asdf

asdf is a versatile version manager that can handle multiple languages, including Ruby, Node.js, Python, and more. It has a steeper learning curve than rbenv, but its versatility can be beneficial if you work with multiple languages.

macOS (using Homebrew):

1. **Install Homebrew (if you haven't already):** (Same as rbenv instructions)
2. **Install asdf:**

```
brew install asdf
```

3. **Configure your shell:** Add the following line to your shell's configuration file (~/.zshrc or ~/.bashrc):

```
. "$HOME/.asdf/asdf.sh"
```

4. **Restart your terminal or source your shell configuration file:** (Same as rbenv instructions)
5. **Add the Ruby plugin:**

```
asdf plugin add ruby https://github.com/asdf-vm/asdf-ruby.git
```

6. **Install a Ruby version:**

```
asdf install ruby 3.2.2
```

7. **Set the global Ruby version:**

```
asdf global ruby 3.2.2
```

8. **Verify the installation:**

```
ruby -v
```

Linux: Follow the instructions on the asdf website (https://asdf-vm.com/guide/getting-started.html) for your specific distribution.

Windows (using WSL): Follow the Linux instructions above within your WSL terminal.

My Personal Tip: Don't be afraid of the command line! It's a powerful tool that you'll use frequently as a web developer. Take the time to learn the basic commands, and you'll be amazed at how much more efficient you become. I used to dread using the terminal, but now I can't imagine developing without it.

Troubleshooting Common Issues:

- **"Command not found":** If you get a "command not found" error after installing rbenv or asdf, make sure you've correctly configured your shell and restarted your terminal or sourced your shell configuration file.
- **Installation errors:** If you encounter errors during the Ruby installation process, make sure you have the necessary dependencies installed. The error message should provide clues about which dependencies are missing.
- **Permission issues:** If you encounter permission issues, try running the commands with sudo (on Linux or macOS).

Code Example (Upcoming):

In the next chapter, we'll start writing Ruby code. I'll provide plenty of examples to help you learn the basics of the language.

Conclusion:

You've now successfully installed Ruby using either rbenv or asdf. This is a crucial step in your web development journey. With Ruby installed, you're ready to move on to the next step: installing Rails! Let's get ready!

2.2 Installing Rails: Your Web Development Framework

With Ruby successfully installed (using rbenv or asdf, congratulations!), it's time to install Rails. Rails, as you now know, is the powerful web application framework that will help you build your web applications quickly and efficiently.

Rails is distributed as a Ruby *gem*. A gem is essentially a packaged library of Ruby code that can be easily installed and used in your projects. Gems encapsulate reusable functionality, allowing you to easily incorporate existing solutions into your applications.

Installing the Rails Gem

The process of installing Rails is surprisingly straightforward. Open your terminal and run the following command:

```
gem install rails -v 8.0.0 # Or the latest Rails 8 version
```

Let's break this down:

- gem: This is the command-line tool for managing Ruby gems. It comes pre-installed with Ruby.
- install: This tells gem to install a gem.
- rails: This specifies that we want to install the Rails gem.
- -v 8.0.0: This specifies the version of Rails we want to install. It's a good practice to specify the version number to ensure you're using the version that the book is based on (or the latest Rails 8 version). If you leave this out, it will install the latest version of Rails, which *might* have compatibility issues.

Understanding Gem Dependencies

When you install a gem, it often has *dependencies* on other gems. The gem command automatically handles these dependencies, installing any required gems along with Rails. This makes the installation process much simpler, as you don't have to manually install each dependency individually.

Important Post-Installation Steps

After installing Rails, there are a couple of important steps you need to take to ensure that your system is configured correctly:

1. **Update your gem executables (rbenv/asdf specific):** This step ensures that your system can find the rails executable. Run the following command:
     o **If you're using rbenv:**

```
rbenv rehash
```

     o **If you're using asdf:**

```
asdf reshim
```

2. This command updates the shell's shims, which are used to locate executable files.

3. **Verify the Installation:** To confirm that Rails is installed correctly, run the following command:

```
rails -v
```

This should output the version of Rails that you installed (e.g., Rails 8.0.0).

Troubleshooting Common Issues

- **"Gem::FilePermissionError":** If you encounter a Gem::FilePermissionError, it means you don't have the necessary permissions to install gems. This is often caused by installing Ruby system-wide (which we avoided by using rbenv or asdf). To fix this, you can try running the gem install command with sudo (on Linux or macOS):

```
sudo gem install rails -v 8.0.0
```

  However, this isn't the *recommended* solution. It's better to configure your Ruby environment to allow you to install gems without sudo. Consult your rbenv or asdf documentation for the best way to do this.

- **"rails command not found":** If you get a "rails command not found" error after installing Rails, it means your system can't find the rails executable. This is usually caused by not running rbenv rehash or asdf reshim after installing Rails. Make sure you run this command, and then try running rails -v again.
- **"Bundler::GemNotFound":** When creating a new Rails application (which we'll do soon), you might encounter an error related to Bundler, the gem dependency manager. This usually means you need to install Bundler: gem install bundler.

My Personal Recommendation: Always read the output of the gem install command carefully. It often provides valuable information about any potential problems or missing dependencies. Also, don't be afraid to search online for solutions if you encounter errors. The Rails community is very active, and chances are someone else has already encountered and solved the same problem.

Code Example (Upcoming)

In the next chapter, we'll use the rails command to create a new Rails application. You'll see firsthand how easy it is to get started with Rails.

Conclusion

You've now successfully installed Rails! You're one step closer to building amazing web applications. In the next section, we'll install and configure PostgreSQL, the database system that we'll be using to store our application's data. Let's keep the momentum going!

2.3 Installing PostgreSQL: Your Data's Home

You've successfully installed Ruby and Rails – fantastic! Now it's time to set up our database. Think of a database as a digital warehouse where your application will store all its important information: user accounts, product details, blog posts, comments, and much more. We'll be using PostgreSQL, a powerful and reliable open-source database system.

Why PostgreSQL? It's robust, standards-compliant, and integrates seamlessly with Rails, making it an excellent choice for both beginners and experienced developers. It's also free and open-source, which is always a plus!

The installation process varies slightly depending on your operating system, so let's cover the most common ones:

macOS (using Homebrew):

1. **Install PostgreSQL:** Open your terminal and run the following command:

   ```
   brew install postgresql
   ```

   This command will download and install PostgreSQL and its dependencies using Homebrew.

2. **Start the PostgreSQL server:** After the installation is complete, you need to start the PostgreSQL server. You can do this by running:

```
brew services start postgresql
```

This command will start the PostgreSQL server in the background, so it will automatically start when you log in to your computer.

Important Note: On macOS, Homebrew installs PostgreSQL with a default configuration. You may need to adjust the configuration settings if you want to customize the way PostgreSQL runs. See the Homebrew documentation for details.

Linux (Debian/Ubuntu - using apt): Adapt these instructions as needed for your specific distribution and package manager (yum, dnf, etc.).

1. **Update your package list:** Before installing PostgreSQL, it's a good practice to update your package list:

```
sudo apt update
```

2. **Install PostgreSQL:**

```
sudo apt install postgresql postgresql-contrib
```

This command will install the PostgreSQL server and the postgresql-contrib package, which contains useful utilities and extensions.

3. **Start and enable the PostgreSQL service:** After the installation is complete, you need to start the PostgreSQL service and enable it to start automatically at boot:

```
sudo systemctl start postgresql
sudo systemctl enable postgresql
```

Windows:

Installing PostgreSQL on Windows requires downloading and running an installer from the official PostgreSQL website.

1. **Download the installer:** Go to the PostgreSQL download page (https://www.postgresql.org/download/windows/) and download the installer for your Windows version.
2. **Run the installer:** Double-click the installer file to start the installation process. Follow the on-screen instructions.
   - **Important:** During the installation, you'll be prompted to set a password for the postgres user. Make sure you choose a strong password and remember it, as you'll need it later to connect to the database. Also, note the port it uses (5432 is the default).
   - The installer will also ask if you want to install pgAdmin 4. pgAdmin is a graphical administration tool for PostgreSQL. It's a helpful tool for managing your database, but it's not required for this book. You can choose to install it or not, depending on your preference.

Verifying the Installation

After installing PostgreSQL, it's a good idea to verify that it's running correctly. You can do this by running the following command in your terminal:

```
psql --version
```

This should output the version of PostgreSQL that you installed. If you get an error message, it means that PostgreSQL is not installed correctly, or it's not in your system's PATH.

Connecting to PostgreSQL (Initial Steps)

Now that you have PostgreSQL installed, you can connect to it using the psql command-line tool.

1. **Open a terminal:**
2. **Connect to the postgres database:**

```
psql -U postgres
```

On Windows, you might need to specify the host: psql -h localhost -U postgres and you'll be prompted for the password you set during installation.

This command will connect you to the postgres database as the postgres user. You'll be presented with a postgres=# prompt.

Important: The postgres user is a superuser account with full privileges. You should only use it for administrative tasks. For your application, you'll create a separate user with limited privileges.

3. **Exit psql:** To exit the psql command-line tool, type \q and press Enter.

Troubleshooting Common Issues

- **"psql: command not found":** If you get a "psql: command not found" error, it means that the psql command-line tool is not in your system's PATH. You may need to add the PostgreSQL bin directory to your PATH.
- **"FATAL: role "yourusername" does not exist":** This error means that PostgreSQL doesn't have a user with your operating system username. This is common on macOS. You can create a user with your username by running:

```
sudo -u postgres createuser -s $USER
```

Then, try connecting to PostgreSQL again using the command psql.

- **Authentication errors:** Double-check that the service is running and that you are using the correct username and password.

My Personal Tip: PostgreSQL can be intimidating at first, but don't let it scare you! The psql command-line tool is your friend. It allows you to explore the database, run SQL queries, and manage your data. Take the time to learn the basic SQL commands, and you'll be well on your way to mastering PostgreSQL.

Code Example (Upcoming)

In the next chapter, we'll create a new Rails application and connect it to our PostgreSQL database. You'll see firsthand how easy it is to interact with PostgreSQL from Rails.

Conclusion

You've successfully installed and configured PostgreSQL! You now have a place to store your application's data. In the next section, we'll configure your code editor to work with Ruby and Rails. Let's keep the momentum going!

2.4 Configuring Your Code Editor: Your Development Command Center

You've installed Ruby, Rails, and PostgreSQL – you're making excellent progress! Now, let's set up your *code editor*. Your code editor is where you'll spend most of your time writing, editing, and debugging code. Choosing the right code editor and configuring it properly can significantly boost your productivity and make the development process more enjoyable.

Think of your code editor as your digital workshop. You want it to be comfortable, well-organized, and equipped with the right tools to make your job easier.

I recommend two excellent code editors: VS Code and Sublime Text. Both are powerful, customizable, and have excellent support for Ruby and Rails development. I'll provide instructions for both, so you can choose the one that best suits your preferences.

VS Code (Free and Highly Recommended)

VS Code (Visual Studio Code) is a free, open-source code editor developed by Microsoft. It's incredibly popular among web developers due to its versatility, extensive extension ecosystem, and excellent support for various programming languages, including Ruby.

Why Choose VS Code?

- **Free and Open Source:** It doesn't cost anything to use, and it's open source, meaning the code is available for anyone to view and modify.

- **Extensive Extension Ecosystem:** VS Code has a vast marketplace of extensions that can add new features and functionality to the editor, such as syntax highlighting, code completion, linting, and debugging.
- **Integrated Terminal:** VS Code has a built-in terminal, allowing you to run commands without leaving the editor.
- **Excellent Git Integration:** VS Code has excellent support for Git, the version control system that we'll be using to track our code changes.
- **Debugging Support:** VS Code has powerful debugging tools that allow you to step through your code, inspect variables, and identify and fix errors.

Configuring VS Code for Rails Development

1. **Download and Install VS Code:** Go to the official VS Code website (https://code.visualstudio.com/) and download the installer for your operating system. Follow the on-screen instructions to install VS Code.
2. **Install Recommended Extensions:** VS Code's power lies in its extensions. Here are some essential extensions for Rails development:
   - **Ruby (by Peng Lv):** Provides syntax highlighting, code completion, linting, and debugging support for Ruby code.
   - **Rails Snippets:** Provides code snippets for common Rails tasks, such as generating models, controllers, and views.
   - **Prettier - Code formatter:** Automatically formats your code to adhere to a consistent style.
   - **EditorConfig for VS Code:** (Optional) Enforces consistent coding styles across multiple developers working on the same project.

   To install an extension, click on the Extensions icon in the Activity Bar (on the left side of the VS Code window), search for the extension by name, and click the "Install" button.

3. **Configure VS Code Settings:** You can customize VS Code's behavior by modifying its settings. Here are some recommended settings for Rails development:
   - **Ruby Linting:** VS Code can use RuboCop, a popular Ruby linting tool, to automatically check your code for style violations and potential errors. To enable RuboCop linting, open the VS Code settings (File -> Preferences -> Settings)

and search for "ruby.lint". Set the "Ruby Lint" setting to "rubocop". You might need to install RuboCop gem in your project, depending on the global settings.

- o **Ruby Formatting:** VS Code can automatically format your Ruby code using a code formatter like Prettier. To enable code formatting, search for "ruby.format" and set the "Ruby Format" setting to "true". You might need to install the Prettier gem and configure it.
- o **Editor: Format On Save:** Configure VS Code to automatically format your code every time you save a file. Search for "editor.formatOnSave" and check the box to enable it.
- o **Files: Auto Save:** Automatically saves every file after a short delay.

Sublime Text (Paid, but with a Free Evaluation)

Sublime Text is a fast, lightweight, and highly customizable code editor. While it's not free (it requires a paid license), it offers a free evaluation period, so you can try it out before committing to a purchase. Many developers swear by Sublime Text for its speed and simplicity.

Why Choose Sublime Text?

- **Speed and Performance:** Sublime Text is known for its exceptional speed and responsiveness, even when working with large files.
- **Minimalist Interface:** Sublime Text has a clean and uncluttered interface that allows you to focus on your code.
- **Powerful Features:** Sublime Text offers a wide range of powerful features, such as multiple selections, command palette, and project management.
- **Extensive Package Ecosystem:** Sublime Text has a large ecosystem of packages that can add new features and functionality to the editor.
- **Cross-Platform:** Sublime Text is available for macOS, Windows, and Linux.

Configuring Sublime Text for Rails Development

1. **Download and Install Sublime Text:** Go to the official Sublime Text website (https://www.sublimetext.com/) and download the installer for your operating system. Follow the on-screen instructions to install Sublime Text.

2. **Install Package Control:** Package Control is a package manager for Sublime Text that simplifies the process of installing and managing packages. To install Package Control, open the Sublime Text console (View -> Show Console) and paste the code from the Package Control website (https://packagecontrol.io/installation) into the console. Press Enter.

3. **Install Recommended Packages:** Once Package Control is installed, you can use it to install essential packages for Rails development:
   - **Ruby Syntax Highlighting:** Provides syntax highlighting for Ruby code.
   - **Rails snippets:** Provides code snippets for common Rails tasks.
   - **RuboCop:** Integrates RuboCop, a popular Ruby linting tool, into Sublime Text.

To install a package, press Ctrl+Shift+P (or Cmd+Shift+P on macOS) to open the Command Palette, type "Install Package," and press Enter. Then, search for the package by name and press Enter to install it.

My Personal Tip: Experiment with different code editors and extensions to find the combination that works best for you. Don't be afraid to try new things and customize your editor to fit your workflow. I've tried many editors over the years, and I've settled on VS Code for its versatility and extensive extension ecosystem. But ultimately, the best code editor is the one that you're most comfortable using.

Code Example (Upcoming)

In the next chapter, when we start writing Ruby and Rails code, you'll see how these editor configurations enhance your coding experience.

Key Takeaways

A properly configured code editor is a crucial tool for any web developer. Take the time to explore the features and extensions of your chosen editor and customize it to fit your needs. A well-configured editor can significantly boost your productivity and make the development process more enjoyable.

2.5 Command-Line Essentials: Your Superpower Tool for Web Development

You've set up your code editor, and now it's time to master another essential tool for web developers: the *command line*. The command line, also known as the terminal or console, is a text-based interface that allows you to interact directly with your computer's operating system.

While it might seem intimidating at first, the command line is incredibly powerful and efficient. It allows you to perform tasks that would be much slower or more difficult using a graphical user interface (GUI). Mastering the command line is a valuable skill that will significantly boost your productivity as a web developer.

Think of the command line as having direct access to your computer's brain. You can give it precise instructions, and it will execute them quickly and accurately.

Why Use the Command Line?

*   **Efficiency:** Many tasks can be performed much faster using the command line than using a GUI.
*   **Automation:** You can automate repetitive tasks by writing shell scripts.
*   **Remote Access:** The command line is essential for working with remote servers.
*   **Version Control:** Git, the version control system we'll be using, is primarily used through the command line.
*   **Essential for Web Development:** Many web development tools, like Rails, are primarily used through the command line.

Opening the Command Line

The way you open the command line depends on your operating system:

*   **macOS:** Open the "Terminal" application, which is located in the /Applications/Utilities folder.
*   **Linux:** Open the "Terminal" application. The name and location may vary depending on your distribution.
*   **Windows:**

- o **Using WSL (Windows Subsystem for Linux):** Open the terminal for your chosen Linux distribution.
- o **Using PowerShell:** Search for "PowerShell" in the Start menu and open it.
- o **Using Command Prompt (cmd.exe):** Search for "Command Prompt" in the Start menu and open it. (PowerShell is generally preferred).

Note: If you're using Windows, I strongly recommend using WSL for web development. It provides a Linux environment that is much closer to the environment used on most web servers, making it easier to deploy your applications.

Essential Command-Line Commands

Let's cover some essential command-line commands that you'll use frequently as a web developer:

- **pwd (Print Working Directory):** This command displays the path to your current directory. It's useful for knowing where you are in the file system.

```
pwd
```

- **cd (Change Directory):** This command allows you to navigate to different directories.
  - o cd <directory>: Changes to the specified directory.
  - o cd ..: Changes to the parent directory.
  - o cd ~: Changes to your home directory.

```
cd Documents
cd ..
cd ~/Projects
```

- **ls (List):** This command lists the files and directories in the current directory.
  - o ls: Lists files and directories.
  - o ls -l: Lists files and directories with detailed information (permissions, size, modification date, etc.).
  - o ls -a: Lists all files and directories, including hidden ones (those starting with a .).

```
        ls
ls -l
ls -a
```

- **mkdir (Make Directory):** This command creates a new directory.

  ```
  mkdir my_new_directory
  ```

- **touch:** (touch a file) creates a new, empty file

  ```
  touch newfile.txt
  ```

- **rm (Remove):** This command deletes files and directories. **Use this command with caution!**
  - rm <file>: Deletes the specified file.
  - rm -r <directory>: Deletes the specified directory and all its contents (recursively).
  - rm -f <file>: Forces the deletion of a file, even if it's write-protected.
  - rm -rf <directory>: Forces the recursive deletion of a directory and all its contents.

  ```
      rm myfile.txt
  rm -r my_old_directory
  ```

- **cp (Copy):** This command copies files and directories.
  - cp <source> <destination>: Copies the source file or directory to the destination.
  - cp -r <source> <destination>: Recursively copies a directory and all its contents.

  ```
      cp myfile.txt mycopy.txt
  cp -r my_directory my_backup_directory
  ```

- **mv (Move):** This command moves (or renames) files and directories.
  - mv <source> <destination>: Moves the source file or directory to the destination, or renames the source if the destination is a file name.

```
     mv myfile.txt newfile.txt  # Renames myfile.txt to
newfile.txt
mv myfile.txt Documents   # Moves myfile.txt to the Documents
directory
```

- **cat (Concatenate):** This command displays the contents of a text file.

```
cat myfile.txt
```

- **echo:** (Echo) displays the text on the terminal.

```
echo "Hello world!"
```

- **clear:** (clear terminal) clear the terminal.

```
clear
```

Understanding Paths

Paths are used to specify the location of files and directories. There are two types of paths:

- **Absolute Paths:** Start with the root directory (/ on macOS and Linux, C:\ on Windows) and specify the exact location of a file or directory. For example, /Users/yourusername/Documents/myfile.txt is an absolute path.
- **Relative Paths:** Specify the location of a file or directory relative to the current directory. For example, if your current directory is /Users/yourusername/Documents, you can access myfile.txt using the relative path myfile.txt.

Tips for Using the Command Line Effectively

- **Use Tab Completion:** Press the Tab key to automatically complete file and directory names. This can save you a lot of typing and prevent errors.
- **Use the History:** Press the Up and Down arrow keys to cycle through your command history. This allows you to easily repeat previous commands.

- **Use Aliases:** Create aliases for frequently used commands. For example, you can create an alias for ls -l to ll by adding the following line to your ~/.zshrc or ~/.bashrc file: alias ll='ls -l'.
- **Practice, Practice, Practice!** The best way to become comfortable with the command line is to use it regularly. Experiment with different commands and try to solve problems using the command line instead of a GUI.

My Personal Transformation: I used to be terrified of the command line. It seemed like a cryptic and unforgiving world. But once I took the time to learn the basics, I realized its power and efficiency. Now, I use the command line for almost everything, from navigating files to managing servers. It's become an indispensable tool in my web development arsenal.

Code Example (Upcoming)

In the next chapter, when we create our first Rails application, you'll use the command line to generate files, run commands, and interact with the Rails server.

Key Takeaways

The command line is an essential tool for web developers. Mastering the basic commands will significantly boost your productivity and open up new possibilities. Don't be afraid to experiment and explore the command line. It's a powerful tool that will serve you well throughout your web development journey.

Chapter 3: Ruby Crash Course for Rails - Your Ruby Toolkit

Congratulations, you've set up your development environment! Now it's time to learn the language that powers Rails: **Ruby**. While you don't need to be a Ruby expert to start building Rails applications, a solid understanding of the basics is essential.

Think of this chapter as your Ruby toolkit. We'll cover the essential Ruby concepts you need to know to get started with Rails, focusing on the aspects that are most relevant to web development. This isn't a comprehensive Ruby course; it's a practical guide to get you up and running quickly.

3.1 Ruby Syntax Basics: Building Blocks of Your Rails Adventures

Before we unleash the power of Rails, let's lay the groundwork with the fundamental syntax of Ruby. It's like learning the alphabet before writing a novel. Understanding variables, data types, and operators will give you the foundation you need to construct elegant and effective Rails applications.

These concepts might seem basic at first, but they are the core of everything you'll do in Ruby. Mastering them early will pay off handsomely as you progress through this book.

Variables: Your Named Containers

In programming, a variable is simply a named storage location that holds a value. Think of it as a labeled box where you can put things for later use. In Ruby, you assign a value to a variable using the assignment operator (=).

```
name = "Alice" # Assigns the string "Alice" to the
variable 'name'
age = 30       # Assigns the integer 30 to the variable 'age'
is_active = true # Assigns the boolean value 'true' to the
variable 'is_active'
```

Key characteristics of Ruby variables:

- **Dynamic Typing:** Ruby is *dynamically typed*, meaning you don't need to explicitly declare the data type of a variable. Ruby infers the type automatically based on the value assigned to it. This makes Ruby code more concise but also requires careful attention to avoid type-related errors.
- **Naming Conventions:** Variable names should start with a lowercase letter or an underscore (_). Use descriptive names that clearly indicate the purpose of the variable. For example, user_name is better than un. Use snake_case (lowercase words separated by underscores) for multi-word variable names.
- **Variable Scope:** The *scope* of a variable determines where it can be accessed in your code. We'll cover variable scope in more detail later, but for now, just be aware that variables defined within a method or block are typically only accessible within that method or block.

Data Types: The Kinds of Values You Can Store

Data types define the kind of values a variable can hold. Ruby provides a rich set of built-in data types, including:

- **Strings:** Represents textual data. Enclosed in single or double quotes.

```
greeting = "Hello, world!"
name = 'John' # Single quotes are generally preferred for
simple strings
```

Strings are incredibly versatile. You can perform operations like concatenation (joining strings together), slicing (extracting parts of a string), and formatting.

- **Integers:** Represents whole numbers (without decimal points).

```
quantity = 10
year = 2023
```

- **Floats:** Represents numbers with decimal points.

```
price = 99.99
temperature = 25.5
```

- **Booleans:** Represents truth values (either true or false).

```
      is_valid = true
is_admin = false
```

- **Symbols:** Represents immutable strings. Symbols are often used as keys in hashes because they are more efficient than strings.

```
:name # A symbol representing the string "name"
:age  # A symbol representing the string "age"
```

Symbols are written with a colon (:) prefix. They are guaranteed to be unique within your application, which makes them ideal for identifying objects or keys.

- **Arrays:** Represents an ordered list of values.

```
numbers = [1, 2, 3, 4, 5]
colors = ["red", "green", "blue"]
```

- **Hashes:** A collection of key-value pairs, where keys are unique.

```
person = { "name" => "Alice", "age" => 30 } # Older
syntax
person = { name: "Alice", age: 30 }  # Preferred shorthand
for symbols as keys

puts person[:name] # Access "name" property of person
```

Hashes are incredibly useful for storing structured data and are used extensively in Rails applications.

Operators: Performing Actions on Data

Operators are special symbols that perform operations on values (operands). Ruby provides a variety of operators:

- **Arithmetic Operators:** Perform mathematical calculations.
    - + (Addition)
    - - (Subtraction)
    - * (Multiplication)
    - / (Division)
    - % (Modulo - returns the remainder of a division)

○ ** (Exponentiation - raises a number to a power)

```
     sum = 10 + 5        # sum is 15
difference = 10 - 5   # difference is 5
product = 10 * 5      # product is 50
quotient = 10 / 5     # quotient is 2
remainder = 10 % 3 # remainder is 1
power = 2 ** 3       # power is 8
```

- **Comparison Operators:** Compare two values and return a boolean result.
    ○ == (Equal to)
    ○ != (Not equal to)
    ○ > (Greater than)
    ○ < (Less than)
    ○ >= (Greater than or equal to)
    ○ <= (Less than or equal to)

```
     10 == 5   #=> false
10 != 5   #=> true
10 > 5    #=> true
10 < 5    #=> false
```

- **Logical Operators:** Combine or modify boolean expressions.
    ○ && (Logical AND) - Returns true only if both operands are true.
    ○ || (Logical OR) - Returns true if at least one operand is true.
    ○ ! (Logical NOT) - Inverts the truth value of an operand.

```
     true && true    #=> true
true && false  #=> false
true || false  #=> true
!true          #=> false
```

- **Assignment Operators:** Assign a value to a variable.
    ○ = (Assignment) - Assigns the value on the right to the variable on the left.
    ○ +=, -=, *=, /=, %= (Compound Assignment) - Perform an operation and assign the result to the variable.

```
     x = 10
x += 5  # Equivalent to x = x + 5 (x is now 15)
```

```
x -= 3   # Equivalent to x = x - 3 (x is now 12)
```

My Personal Tip: When I was learning Ruby, I found it helpful to experiment with these operators in the irb (Interactive Ruby) console. Just type irb in your terminal to launch the console, and then you can try out different expressions and see the results immediately.

Practical Application in Rails (Coming Soon!)

These fundamental concepts will be used extensively throughout this book as we build our Rails applications. You'll use variables to store data, data types to represent different kinds of information, and operators to manipulate data and perform calculations.

The Takeaway:

Understanding variables, data types, and operators is crucial for writing effective Ruby code. These are the fundamental building blocks that you'll use to construct everything from simple scripts to complex web applications. Master these concepts, and you'll be well-prepared for your Rails journey.

3.2 Control Flow: Guiding Your Ruby Code's Path

You've learned the basic building blocks of Ruby: variables, data types, and operators. Now, let's explore how to control the *flow* of your code – how to tell Ruby which parts of your code to execute and when. This is where control flow statements come in.

Think of control flow as the traffic lights and road signs of your code. They guide the execution of your program, allowing you to make decisions, repeat actions, and handle different scenarios.

Ruby provides several powerful control flow statements: if/else, loops (while, until, for, each), and case statements. Mastering these tools will allow you to write dynamic and responsive applications.

if/else Statements: Making Decisions

if/else statements allow you to execute different blocks of code based on a condition. The basic structure is:

```
      if condition
  # Code to execute if the condition is true
else
  # Code to execute if the condition is false
end
```

- condition: An expression that evaluates to either true or false.
- if: Keyword that starts the if statement.
- else: (Optional) Keyword that specifies the code to execute if the condition is false.

Example:

```
      age = 20

if age >= 18
  puts "You are an adult."
else
  puts "You are not an adult yet."
end
```

You can also use the elsif (or elsif) keyword to check multiple conditions:

```
      grade = "B"

if grade == "A"
  puts "Excellent!"
elsif grade == "B"
  puts "Good job!"
elsif grade == "C"
  puts "You passed."
else
  puts "Needs improvement."
end
```

Important Notes:

- The end keyword is essential to mark the end of the if/else statement.
- Ruby considers false and nil (a special value representing the absence of a value) to be "falsy" values. Everything else is considered "truthy."

Loops: Repeating Actions

Loops allow you to execute a block of code repeatedly. Ruby offers several types of loops, each suited for different situations.

- **while Loop:** Executes a block of code as long as a condition is true.

```
    i = 0
while i < 5
  puts i
  i += 1
end
```

Make sure the condition eventually becomes false, otherwise, your loop will run forever (an infinite loop!).

- **until Loop:** Executes a block of code *until* a condition becomes true. It's the opposite of the while loop.

```
    i = 0
until i >= 5
  puts i
  i += 1
end
```

- **for Loop:** Iterates over a range of values or a collection.

```
    for i in 0..4 # i will take on value between 0 to 4,
inclusive
  puts i
end

#Iterating over an array
my_array = ["apple", "banana", "cherry"]
for fruit in my_array
  puts fruit
end
```

- **each Method:** A more Ruby-esque way to iterate over arrays and hashes. It's a *method* that's called on the collection.

```
    numbers = [1, 2, 3, 4, 5]
numbers.each do |number|
  puts number * 2  # Prints each number multiplied by 2
end
```

```
#Iterating over a Hash
person = {name: "Alice", age: 30}
person.each do |key, value|
  puts "#{key}: #{value}" # Prints "name: Alice", "age: 30"
end
```

The each method is generally preferred in Ruby because it's more concise and expressive. The |number| (or |key, value| for hashes) is called a *block* - a chunk of code that's passed to the each method to be executed for each element.

case Statements: Handling Multiple Scenarios

case statements provide a concise way to handle multiple possible values of a variable. It's like a more powerful version of the if/elsif/else statement.

```
      day = "Monday"

case day
when "Monday"
  puts "Start of the week"
when "Friday"
  puts "Almost the weekend!"
when "Saturday", "Sunday" # Grouping multiple values
  puts "Weekend!"
else
  puts "Just another day."
end
```

The case statement evaluates the expression (day in this case) and compares it to each when clause. If a match is found, the corresponding code is executed. The else clause is executed if no match is found.

My "Learning Curve" Story: I initially found the sheer number of looping options in Ruby a bit overwhelming. But once I realized that each is the preferred approach for most situations, things became much clearer. The each method with its associated block allows for elegant, readable iterations, especially when working with arrays and hashes.

Practical Applications in Rails (Coming Up!)

These control flow statements are essential for building dynamic web applications. You'll use them to:

- Display different content based on user roles.
- Iterate over lists of data from your database.
- Handle form submissions and validate user input.
- And much more!

The Takeaway:

Mastering control flow is key to writing flexible and powerful Ruby code. Experiment with these statements, try different scenarios, and get comfortable with choosing the right tool for the job. These control structures will form the backbone of your logic as you build Rails applications. They enable you to write code that responds intelligently to a wide variety of conditions and inputs.

3.3 Methods and Object-Oriented Programming (OOP): Structuring Your Ruby World

You've grasped the basics of Ruby syntax and control flow. Now, let's step into the world of *methods* and *object-oriented programming* (OOP), which are essential for building organized and maintainable Ruby code, and especially important for working with Rails.

Think of methods as reusable blocks of code that perform specific tasks, and OOP as a way to structure your code around "objects" that represent real-world entities. Understanding these concepts will allow you to write more modular, flexible, and scalable applications.

Methods: Reusable Code Blocks

A method is a named block of code that performs a specific task. Methods allow you to break down complex problems into smaller, more manageable chunks. You define a method using the def keyword, followed by the method name and any parameters it accepts.

```ruby
    def greet(name)
  puts "Hello, #{name}!"
end

greet("Alice")   # Output: Hello, Alice!
greet("Bob")     # Output: Hello, Bob!
```

- def: Keyword to define a method.
- greet: The name of the method. Choose descriptive names.
- (name): The parameters the method accepts. In this case, it accepts one parameter called name.
- puts "Hello, #{name}!": The code that the method executes. The #{name} is called string interpolation, where we embed the value of the variable name into the string.
- end: Keyword to mark the end of the method definition.

Methods can also *return* values using the return keyword. If you don't explicitly use return, the last expression evaluated in the method is automatically returned.

```
    def add(x, y)
  x + y  # Last expression, so it's implicitly returned
end

result = add(5, 3) # Output: 8
puts result

def multiply(x, y)
  return x * y # Explicitly returns the result
end

result = multiply(5, 3) # Output: 15
puts result
```

Object-Oriented Programming (OOP): Modeling the World with Objects

OOP is a programming paradigm that structures code around "objects," which are instances of *classes*. Think of a class as a blueprint for creating objects. Classes define the *attributes* (data) and *methods* (behavior) that objects of that class will have.

Key OOP Concepts:

- **Class:** A blueprint or template for creating objects.
- **Object:** An instance of a class.
- **Attributes:** Data that describes an object (also known as instance variables).
- **Methods:** Actions that an object can perform.

Example: Let's model a Dog object:

```
      class Dog
  def initialize(name, breed) #Constructor method
    @name = name         # instance variable representing name
    @breed = breed       # instance variable representing
breed
  end

  def bark #instance method
    puts "Woof!"
  end

  def display_info #instance method
    puts "Name: #{@name}, Breed: #{@breed}"
  end
end

my_dog = Dog.new("Buddy", "Golden Retriever") #create an
instance
my_dog.bark            # Output: Woof!
my_dog.display_info    # Output: Name: Buddy, Breed: Golden
Retriever
```

Let's break down this example:

- class Dog: Defines a class named Dog.
- def initialize(name, breed): This is the *constructor* method. It's called when you create a new Dog object. The initialize method takes two parameters: name and breed.
- @name = name and @breed = breed: These are *instance variables*. They store the name and breed of the dog for that *particular* Dog object. The @ symbol indicates that they are instance variables. Instance variables hold data specific to that object.
- def bark and def display_info: These are *methods* that define the behavior of the Dog class. bark makes the dog woof, and display_info displays the dog's name and breed.
- my_dog = Dog.new("Buddy", "Golden Retriever"): Creates a new Dog object named my_dog, with the name "Buddy" and the breed "Golden Retriever". Dog.new calls the initialize method of the Dog class.
- my_dog.bark and my_dog.display_info: Call the bark and display_info methods on the my_dog object.

Key OOP Principles (Briefly):

- **Encapsulation:** Bundling data (attributes) and methods that operate on that data within a class. This helps protect the data from outside access and modification.
- **Abstraction:** Hiding complex implementation details and exposing only the essential information to the user.
- **Inheritance:** Allows you to create new classes based on existing classes, inheriting their attributes and methods.
- **Polymorphism:** Allows objects of different classes to respond to the same method call in different ways.

We'll explore these principles in more detail as we progress through the book.

My Personal Insight: I remember when OOP finally "clicked" for me. It wasn't just about syntax; it was about *thinking* in terms of objects and their relationships. It's a powerful way to model real-world problems in code. Designing the "Dog" class and giving it attributes and actions was one of my first steps to OOP success.

Practical Applications in Rails (Coming Soon!)

OOP is fundamental to Rails development. Rails models, controllers, and views are all classes. Understanding OOP will help you write more organized, maintainable, and reusable Rails code. You'll use classes to model your application's data (e.g., User, Product, Post), and you'll use methods to define the behavior of those objects.

The Takeaway:

Methods and OOP are essential concepts for any Ruby developer, and especially for Rails developers. Mastering these concepts will allow you to write more organized, maintainable, and scalable applications. So, take the time to understand the principles of OOP, and you'll be well-prepared for your Rails journey.

3.4 Working with Arrays, Hashes, and Strings: Your Data Wrangling Toolkit

You've learned about methods and object-oriented programming – excellent! Now, let's dive into some fundamental data structures that you'll use constantly in your Ruby and Rails applications: **Arrays, Hashes, and Strings**.

These data structures are your tools for organizing, manipulating, and representing data. Mastering them is essential for building dynamic and interactive web applications. Think of them as your data wrangling toolkit, allowing you to store, retrieve, and transform information efficiently.

Arrays: Ordered Collections of Data

An array is an ordered collection of objects. Think of it as a list where the order of the elements matters. You create an array using square brackets [].

```
    numbers = [1, 2, 3, 4, 5]  # An array of integers
colors = ["red", "green", "blue"] # An array of strings
mixed = [1, "hello", true, 3.14] # Arrays can contain mixed
data types

puts numbers[0] # Access element at index 0 (output: 1)
puts colors[2]  # Access element at index 2 (output: blue)
```

Key array features:

- **Indexing:** Elements in an array are accessed using their index, starting from 0 for the first element. Negative indices can be used to access elements from the end of the array (e.g., numbers[-1] refers to the last element).
- **Mutability:** Arrays are mutable, meaning you can change their contents after they are created.
- **Dynamic Size:** Arrays can grow or shrink dynamically as you add or remove elements.

Common Array Methods:

Arrays provide a rich set of methods for manipulating data. Here are some of the most commonly used ones:

- push(element) or << element: Adds an element to the end of the array.

```
    numbers = [1, 2, 3]
numbers.push(4)  # numbers is now [1, 2, 3, 4]
numbers << 5     # numbers is now [1, 2, 3, 4, 5]
```

- pop: Removes and returns the last element of the array.

```
    numbers = [1, 2, 3]
last_element = numbers.pop  # last_element is 3, numbers is
now [1, 2]
```

- shift: Removes and returns the first element of the array.

```
    numbers = [1, 2, 3]
first_element = numbers.shift # first_element is 1, numbers
is now [2, 3]
```

- unshift(element): Adds an element to the beginning of the array.

```
    numbers = [2, 3]
numbers.unshift(1)   # numbers is now [1, 2, 3]
```

- length or size: Returns the number of elements in the array.

```
    numbers = [1, 2, 3]
puts numbers.length # Output: 3
```

- each: Iterates over the elements of the array, executing a block of code for each element.

```
    numbers = [1, 2, 3]
numbers.each do |number|
  puts number * 2
end #Output: 2, 4, 6
```

- map: Creates a new array by applying a block of code to each element of the original array.

```
    numbers = [1, 2, 3]
doubled_numbers = numbers.map { |number| number * 2 }
puts doubled_numbers # Output: [2, 4, 6]
```

- select: Creates a new array containing only the elements that satisfy a given condition.

```
    numbers = [1, 2, 3, 4, 5]
even_numbers = numbers.select { |number| number % 2 == 0 }
puts even_numbers  # Output: [2, 4]
```

Hashes: Key-Value Pairs

A hash is a collection of key-value pairs. Think of it as a dictionary where you can look up values using their associated keys. You create a hash using curly braces {}.

```
    person = { "name" => "Alice", "age" => 30, "city" =>
"New York" } # Older Syntax

person = { name: "Alice", age: 30, city: "New York" }
#Preferred modern Syntax

puts person[:name]  # Access the value associated with the
key :name (Output: Alice)
puts person[:age]   # Access the value associated with the
key :age (Output: 30)
```

Key Hash features:

- **Keys:** Keys must be unique within a hash. They can be strings, symbols, or other objects. Symbols are generally preferred for keys because they are more efficient.
- **Values:** Values can be any Ruby object.
- **Mutability:** Hashes are mutable, meaning you can add, remove, or modify key-value pairs after the hash is created.
- **Unordered (generally):** Hashes are generally unordered, meaning the order in which the key-value pairs are stored is not guaranteed.

Common Hash Methods:

- []= (Assignment): Adds a new key-value pair to the hash or updates the value of an existing key.

```
    person = { name: "Alice" }
person[:age] = 30 #Adds a property
person[:name] = "Bob" #Changes a property
```

58

```
puts person    # Output: {:name=>"Bob", :age=>30}
```

- delete(key): Removes the key-value pair associated with the specified key.

```
person = { name: "Alice", age: 30 }
person.delete(:age)
puts person    # Output: {:name=>"Alice"}
```

- keys: Returns an array of all the keys in the hash.

```
person = { name: "Alice", age: 30 }
puts person.keys    # Output: [:name, :age]
```

- values: Returns an array of all the values in the hash.

```
person = { name: "Alice", age: 30 }
puts person.values    # Output: ["Alice", 30]
```

- each: Iterates over the key-value pairs in the hash, executing a block of code for each pair.

```
person = { name: "Alice", age: 30 }
person.each do |key, value|
  puts "#{key}: #{value}"
end # Outputs: name: Alice, age: 30
```

Strings: Sequences of Characters

A string is a sequence of characters. You create a string using single or double quotes.

```
message = "Hello, world!"
name = 'Jane'
```

String Interpolation: Double quotes allow you to use string interpolation, which lets you embed the value of variables directly into the string.

59

```
    name = "Alice"
greeting = "Hello, #{name}!"  # greeting is now "Hello,
Alice!"
puts greeting
```

Single quotes treat the string literally, so interpolation doesn't work.

Common String Methods:

- length: Returns the number of characters in the string.

```
    message = "Hello"
puts message.length # Output: 5
```

- upcase: Returns a new string with all characters converted to uppercase.

```
    message = "hello"
puts message.upcase # Output: HELLO
```

- downcase: Returns a new string with all characters converted to lowercase.

```
    message = "HELLO"
puts message.downcase  # Output: hello
```

- strip: Returns a new string with leading and trailing whitespace removed.

```
    message = "   Hello, world!   "
puts message.strip  # Output: Hello, world!
```

- split(delimiter): Splits the string into an array of substrings, using the specified delimiter.

```
    message = "Hello, world!"
words = message.split(", ")  # words is now ["Hello",
"world!"]
puts words
```

- include?(substring): Returns true if the string contains the specified substring, false otherwise.

```
message = "Hello, world!"
puts message.include?("world") # Output: true
puts message.include?("Rails") # Output: false
```

My Experience: I remember the first time I used a hash to store data in a Rails application. It was a revelation! Hashes provide a clean and organized way to represent data, and they make it easy to access specific values by name. It truly was a turning point in my understanding of structuring applications.

Practical Applications in Rails (Coming Soon!)

Arrays, hashes, and strings are used extensively in Rails applications. You'll use them to:

- Store data retrieved from a database.
- Represent user input from forms.
- Manipulate text and data in your views.
- Create and process JSON data for APIs.
- Pass values to methods and display properties on pages.

The Takeaway:

Arrays, hashes, and strings are essential data structures that you'll use constantly in your Ruby and Rails applications. Mastering these tools will allow you to store, retrieve, and transform data efficiently, enabling you to build dynamic and interactive web applications. So, practice working with these data structures, and you'll be well-prepared for your Rails journey!

3.5 Essential Ruby Gems: Supercharging Your Rails Applications

You've laid the foundation with Ruby syntax, data structures, and OOP principles. Now, let's explore a key element of the Ruby and Rails ecosystem: **Gems**. Gems are pre-packaged libraries of Ruby code that extend the functionality of your applications. They're like pre-built components that you can easily plug into your projects to add features without having to write everything from scratch.

Think of gems as ready-made superpowers for your Rails application. They can save you countless hours of development time and provide access to powerful features that would be difficult or impossible to implement on your own.

In this section, we'll cover some essential Ruby gems that are commonly used in Rails development. These gems will help you manage dependencies, debug your code, test your application, and generate realistic data.

Bundler: Managing Your Gem Dependencies

Bundler is a gem dependency manager. It ensures that your application uses the correct versions of all its dependencies. Bundler is already included in your Rails application by default, so you don't need to install it separately.

Bundler uses a file called Gemfile to specify the gems that your application depends on. The Gemfile is located in the root directory of your Rails application. When you run the bundle install command, Bundler reads the Gemfile and installs all the specified gems and their dependencies.

```
    # Gemfile

source 'https://rubygems.org' #Source to download gems

gem 'rails', '~> 8.0' #Declares the rail gem, can specify the
version or use `~>` to allow minor updates
gem 'pg' #postgres database adapter, used to connect to your
database
# Other gems will go here
```

Key Bundler commands:

- bundle install: Installs all the gems listed in the Gemfile.
- bundle update: Updates all the gems listed in the Gemfile to their latest versions.
- bundle exec <command>: Executes a command in the context of your application's gem environment. This ensures that you're using the correct versions of the gems.

Pry: Supercharged Interactive Debugging

Pry is an alternative to the standard irb (Interactive Ruby) console. Pry provides a more powerful and feature-rich debugging environment. It allows you to inspect variables, step through code, and even modify code on the fly.

To install Pry, add the following line to your Gemfile:

```
      #Gemfile
group :development, :test do
  gem 'pry-rails' #Pry-rails automatically loads pry in your
rails environment
end
```

Then, run bundle install.

Key Pry features:

- binding.pry: Inserts a breakpoint into your code. When the code reaches the binding.pry statement, Pry will launch and allow you to inspect the current state of your application.
- ls: Lists the variables and methods available in the current scope.
- cd: Changes the current object context.
- show-source: Displays the source code of a method.

RuboCop: Enforcing Ruby Style and Best Practices

RuboCop is a static code analyzer and formatter that helps you follow Ruby style guidelines and avoid common errors. It enforces a consistent coding style across your project, making your code more readable and maintainable.

To install RuboCop, add the following line to your Gemfile:

```
      #Gemfile
group :development do
  gem 'rubocop', require: false
end
```

Then, run bundle install.

To run RuboCop, use the following command:

```
      bundle exec rubocop
```

RuboCop will analyze your code and report any style violations or potential errors. You can configure RuboCop to automatically fix many of these issues using the rubocop -a command.

Faker: Generating Realistic Fake Data

Faker is a gem that generates realistic fake data for testing and development. It can generate names, addresses, phone numbers, email addresses, and much more. Faker is incredibly useful for populating your database with realistic data for testing purposes.

To install Faker, add the following line to your Gemfile:

```
#Gemfile
group :development, :test do
  gem 'faker'
end
```

Then, run bundle install.

Here are some examples of using Faker:

```
require 'faker'

Faker::Name.name        #=> "Christy Roberts"
Faker::Internet.email   #=> "nikolai.romaguera@jast.net"
Faker::Address.city     #=> "Amityville"
```

RSpec: Testing Your Rails Applications

RSpec is a popular testing framework for Ruby and Rails. It provides a clear and expressive syntax for writing tests, and it helps you ensure that your application is working correctly. We'll dedicate a later chapter to testing, but it's important to know about RSpec now.

To install RSpec, add the following lines to your Gemfile:

```
#Gemfile
group :development, :test do
  gem 'rspec-rails'
end
```

Then, run bundle install.

Other Notable Gems

This is just a small sampling of the many useful Ruby gems available. As you become more experienced with Rails, you'll discover many other gems that can help you solve specific problems and enhance your applications. Here are a few other notable gems:

- **dotenv:** Loads environment variables from a .env file.
- **bcrypt:** For encrypting passwords.
- **kaminari:** A popular pagination engine.
- **image_processing:** A gem for processing images.

My "Gem Discovery" Experience: I remember the first time I discovered the Faker gem. It was a game-changer for populating my development databases with realistic data. Before Faker, I was manually typing in fake names, addresses, and email addresses, which was incredibly tedious. Faker saved me countless hours of work.

The Takeaway:

Ruby gems are an essential part of the Rails ecosystem. They provide pre-built components that can save you time and effort and extend the functionality of your applications. Take the time to explore the available gems and learn how to use them effectively. Gems are what makes Rails development so quick and simple. As you progress through the book, you'll have many opportunities to use these gems in practice.

Chapter 4: Your First Rails Application - Launching Your Web Dev Journey!

You've conquered the initial setup and learned some Ruby fundamentals. Now, it's time for the exciting part: creating your first Rails application! This is where all your preparation comes together, and you'll see the power of Rails in action.

Think of this chapter as launching your web development rocket. We'll take you from zero to a running Rails application in just a few steps. It's going to be a blast!

4.1 Creating a New Rails Project: Your Adventure Begins!

The rails new command is the magic spell that conjures up a brand-new Rails application. It's the foundation upon which all your web development adventures will be built. Understanding how to use this command effectively is the first step towards becoming a confident Rails developer.

This command isn't just about generating files; it's about setting up the structure and environment for a well-organized and maintainable application. Think of it as laying the foundation for a sturdy building, ensuring everything is properly aligned and ready for construction.

The rails new Command: A Detailed Look

The basic syntax for the rails new command is:

```
rails new <application_name> [options]
```

Let's break down the components:

- rails new: This invokes the Rails application generator.
- <application_name>: This is the name of your application. It should be a valid directory name. Choose a descriptive name that reflects the purpose of your project (e.g., blog, ecommerce, task_manager).

- [options]: These are optional flags that modify the behavior of the rails new command. We'll explore some of the most important options below.

Key Options for rails new

While the rails new command has many options, here are some of the most essential ones you'll use frequently:

- --database=postgresql: Specifies the database adapter to use. By default, Rails uses SQLite, which is fine for development but not recommended for production. We strongly recommend using PostgreSQL, as it's more robust and scalable.
- -T or --skip-test: Skips the creation of the default test suite (Minitest). While testing is crucial, we'll cover testing in a later chapter. For now, you can skip the default test suite to keep things simple. We will, however, use RSpec later.
- --api: Creates an API-only application, which is designed for building backends that serve data to front-end applications or mobile apps. This option omits the default views and assets.
- -j <javascript bundler> or --javascript=<javascript bundler>: Configures the JavaScript bundler to use. Common options include webpacker (the default), esbuild, and importmap. This is how you control if you want to use webpacker (which comes with more setup, but is easier to use with external javascript libraries) or use esbuild/importmap which has less setup but more involved configuration of external javascript libraries.
- -c <css bundler> or --css=<css bundler>: Configures the CSS bundler to use. Common options include tailwind, bootstrap, bulma, and sass. This is how you can install tailwind or bootstrap css into your application at the onset.

Putting it into Practice: Creating Your First Rails Application

Let's create a new Rails application called my_awesome_app using PostgreSQL as the database:

```
rails new my_awesome_app --database=postgresql
```

Alternatively, if you also want to skip the default test suite, configure Tailwind CSS, and use Importmap for Javascript:

```
rails new my_awesome_app --database=postgresql -T -c
tailwind -j importmap
```

Steps to Create Your App:

1. **Open your terminal:** Navigate to the directory where you want to create your Rails application. For example, you might create a Projects directory in your home directory:

```
cd ~
mkdir Projects
cd Projects
```

2. **Run the rails new command:** Execute the command with your chosen options.
3. **Wait for the process to complete:** Rails will generate a lot of files and directories. This process may take a few minutes, depending on your computer's speed and internet connection.
4. **Navigate to your application directory:** Once the process is complete, change your directory to the newly created application directory:

```
cd my_awesome_app
```

Common Mistakes and Troubleshooting

- **PostgreSQL not installed:** If you get an error related to PostgreSQL, make sure you have PostgreSQL installed and running on your system. See the previous chapter for instructions.
- **Incorrect database credentials:** If you get a database connection error, check your config/database.yml file to ensure that the database credentials (username, password, database name) are correct.
- **Gems not installed:** If you encounter errors related to missing gems, run bundle install to install the required dependencies.

My Personal Best Practice: I always specify the database adapter when creating a new Rails application. Even if I'm just building a small prototype, it's a good habit to get into, as it avoids potential issues down the road. I also tend to use the -T flag (skip tests) initially and set up RSpec later.

Key Takeaways:

- The rails new command is the starting point for any Rails project.
- Choose a descriptive name for your application.
- Use the --database=postgresql option to specify PostgreSQL as the database adapter.
- Use other options to customize the application generation process, as needed.
- Be patient and troubleshoot any errors that may arise.

With your new Rails application created, you're ready to explore the project structure and start building amazing things! Get ready to dive deeper into the world of Rails!

4.2 Decoding the Rails Project Structure: Your Application's DNA

You've successfully created a new Rails application using the rails new command – excellent! But now you're faced with a multitude of files and directories. Don't panic! The Rails project structure is well-organized and follows a clear set of conventions. Understanding this structure is crucial for navigating your application, finding the code you need, and maintaining a clean and organized codebase.

Think of the Rails project structure as the DNA of your application. Each directory and file has a specific purpose, and together they define the overall structure and behavior of your application.

A Guided Tour of the Rails Project

Let's take a guided tour of the key directories and files in a Rails project:

- **app/:** This is the heart of your application. It contains the core logic that defines its behavior.
  - **app/models/:** Contains the *models*, which represent the data in your application. Models interact with the database to retrieve, create, update, and delete data. Each model typically corresponds to a table in your database (e.g., User, Product, Post).

- **app/views/:** Contains the *views*, which are responsible for rendering the user interface. Views are typically written in HTML with embedded Ruby code (ERB) to dynamically generate content. They present the data from your models to the user.
- **app/controllers/:** Contains the *controllers*, which handle user requests and coordinate between models and views. Controllers receive requests from the browser, interact with the models to retrieve or modify data, and then render a view to display the results to the user.
- **app/helpers/:** Contains *helper* modules, which provide reusable view logic. Helpers can simplify your views by encapsulating complex or repetitive code.
- **app/assets/:** Contains the *assets* (images, stylesheets, JavaScript files) used in your application. Rails uses the asset pipeline to manage these assets, allowing you to combine, minify, and compress them for optimal performance.
- **app/channels/:** Contains the Action Cable channels, which are used for real-time communication between the server and the client.
- **config/:** This directory contains configuration files for your application.
  - **config/routes.rb:** Defines the *routes*, which map URLs to controller actions. This file is the roadmap of your application, determining how different URLs are handled.
  - **config/database.yml:** Configures the database connection, specifying the database adapter, hostname, username, password, and database name.
  - **config/environment.rb:** Loads the Rails application and sets up the environment.
  - **config/environments/:** Contains environment-specific configuration files (e.g., development.rb, test.rb, production.rb).
  - **config/initializers/:** Contains initialization files that are loaded when the application starts up. You can use these files to configure various aspects of your application.
  - **config/locales/:** Contains localization files, which are used to translate your application into different languages.
- **db/:** This directory contains files related to the database.
  - **db/migrate/:** Contains the *migrations*, which are used to create and modify the database schema. Migrations allow you

to evolve your database structure over time in a controlled and repeatable way.

- o **db/seeds.rb:** Contains code to seed the database with initial data.
- **lib/:** This directory contains custom libraries and modules that you can use in your application.
  - o This is where you put code that is more complex than helpers, or code that is shared by multiple parts of your application.
- **log/:** This directory contains log files, which record information about your application's activity. Log files are invaluable for debugging and troubleshooting.
- **public/:** This directory contains static files that are served directly to the browser, such as HTML files, images, and JavaScript files.
- **test/:** This directory contains the tests for your application.
  - o This is where you put the models, system, integration and controller tests to ensure all your components work as they are supposed to.
- **vendor/:** This directory contains third-party libraries and plugins.
  - o This directory is for vendoring dependencies (instead of using gems) if you are using javascript bundlers other than webpacker
- **Root Directory Files:**
  - o **Gemfile:** Specifies the gem dependencies for your application. Bundler uses this file to install the required gems.
  - o **Rakefile:** Defines tasks that can be run using the rake command-line tool. Rake is used for automating various tasks, such as running tests, migrating the database, and deploying your application.
  - o **README.md:** Provides information about your application, including installation instructions, usage examples, and contribution guidelines. This is the first thing people will see when visiting your application repository on GitHub or GitLab.

Convention Over Configuration: The Rails Philosophy

The Rails project structure is based on the principle of "convention over configuration." This means that Rails makes intelligent assumptions about how you want to structure your application, reducing the amount of configuration you need to write. By following these conventions, you can focus on the unique aspects of your application, rather than getting bogged down in boilerplate code.

This is what allows Rails projects to be easy to maintain and understand from project to project. Each Rails project will generally follow these conventions.

My Personal Journey: I remember feeling overwhelmed when I first encountered the Rails project structure. But as I started to build applications, I realized the beauty and power of the Rails conventions. The well-defined structure made it easy to find the code I needed, and the consistent organization made it easier to collaborate with other developers.

Key Takeaways:

- The Rails project structure is well-organized and follows a clear set of conventions.
- The app/ directory contains the core logic of your application.
- The config/ directory contains configuration files.
- The db/ directory contains files related to the database.
- The Gemfile specifies the gem dependencies for your application.
- The principle of "convention over configuration" makes Rails development more efficient.

Understanding the Rails project structure is essential for navigating your application and building well-organized and maintainable code. Take the time to explore the different directories and files, and you'll be well-prepared for your Rails journey.

4.3 The Gemfile and Bundler: Your Application's Recipe Book

You've explored the overall structure of a Rails application. Now let's zoom in on a critical component: the Gemfile and its partner in crime, **Bundler**. These tools are essential for managing your application's dependencies, ensuring that it uses the correct versions of all the necessary libraries.

Think of the Gemfile as your application's recipe book. It lists all the ingredients (gems) that your application needs to run. Bundler is the chef who follows the recipe, gathering the ingredients and making sure they're all the right kind and amount.

What is a Gem, Anyway?

A gem, in the Ruby world, is a packaged library of reusable code. It's a way to share and distribute code among developers. Gems provide functionality ranging from simple utilities to complex frameworks, allowing you to easily add features to your applications without having to write everything from scratch. We touched on this in a prior chapter.

The Gemfile: Your Dependency Declaration

The Gemfile is a file located in the root directory of your Rails application. It lists all the gems that your application depends on. The Gemfile uses a simple and declarative syntax:

```
source 'https://rubygems.org' #Location to download gems

git_source(:github) { |repo| "https://github.com/#{repo}.git" } #Optional: A source to load gems from github

ruby '3.2.2' # or similar. Specifies the Ruby version to use for the project.

gem 'rails', '~> 8.0' # The gem 'rails', and use a version ~> 8.0

# Other gems will go here
gem 'bcrypt', '~> 3.1' #Gem to help with encrypting passwords.

group :development, :test do #Group to include gems only for testing/development
  gem 'pry-rails' #Debugging tool
end
```

Let's break down the key elements:

- source 'https://rubygems.org' : This line specifies the primary source for downloading gems. RubyGems.org is the official gem repository.
- git_source(:github) { |repo| "https://github.com/#{repo}.git" }: This line defines a source for gems that are hosted on GitHub. It allows you to specify gems directly from a GitHub repository.
- ruby '3.2.2': Specifies the Ruby version the application is designed for. This helps ensure compatibility.
- gem 'rails', '~> 8.0' : This line declares a dependency on the rails gem, specifying that you want version 8.0 or higher, but less than 8.1. The ~> operator (also known as the pessimistic version constraint) allows

for minor version updates (e.g., 8.0.1, 8.0.2), but not major version updates (e.g., 9.0). This ensures that your application remains compatible with the specified gem, while still benefiting from bug fixes and minor improvements.

- group :development, :test do ... end : This block defines a group of gems that are only needed in the development and test environments. Gems in this group are not installed in the production environment. This is useful for gems that are only used for debugging or testing, such as pry-rails or rspec-rails.
- **Gem Versioning:**
  - 'gem_name' No version specified: It will use the latest version
  - 'gem_name', '1.2.3' Specific version of the gem
  - 'gem_name', '> 1.2.3' Version higher than the version specified.
  - 'gem_name', '< 1.2.3' Version lower than the version specified.
  - 'gem_name', '~> 1.2.3' Version 1.2.x higher or equal to 1.2.3
  - 'gem_name', '>= 1.2.3' Version equal or higher than the version specified
  - 'gem_name', '<= 1.2.3' Version equal or lower than the version specified

Bundler: Your Dependency Manager

Bundler is a gem that manages your application's dependencies. It reads the Gemfile, resolves the dependencies, and installs the required gems. Bundler also creates a Gemfile.lock file, which records the exact versions of all the gems that were installed. This ensures that everyone working on the project uses the same versions of the gems, preventing compatibility issues.

Key Bundler commands:

- bundle install: Installs all the gems listed in the Gemfile. This command should be run whenever you add, remove, or update gems in your Gemfile.

```
bundle install
```

- bundle update: Updates all the gems listed in the Gemfile to their latest versions, while respecting the version constraints specified in the Gemfile. Be careful with this command, as it can potentially

74

break your application if the updated gems introduce compatibility issues.

```
bundle update
```

- bundle exec <command>: Executes a command in the context of your application's gem environment. This ensures that you're using the correct versions of the gems. You should use bundle exec whenever you run commands that depend on gems, such as rails server, rails console, or rake db:migrate.

```
bundle exec rails server
bundle exec rails console
bundle exec rake db:migrate
```

While it is best practice to use bundle exec for every command as suggested, for the Rails command, you only need to run rails s, rails c, rails db:migrate after using rbenv rehash (or asdf reshim)

The Gemfile.lock: Your Dependency Snapshot

The Gemfile.lock file is a critical component of Bundler. It records the exact versions of all the gems that were installed when you ran bundle install. This file ensures that everyone working on the project uses the same versions of the gems, preventing compatibility issues.

Never modify the Gemfile.lock file manually! It is automatically updated by Bundler when you run bundle install or bundle update.

Best Practices for Dependency Management

- **Always use Bundler:** Never install gems directly without using Bundler.
- **Commit the Gemfile.lock file:** Always commit the Gemfile.lock file to your version control system (e.g., Git). This ensures that everyone working on the project uses the same versions of the gems.
- **Run bundle install after making changes to the Gemfile:** Whenever you add, remove, or update gems in your Gemfile, always run bundle install to update your application's gem environment.

- **Use bundle exec to run commands:** Use bundle exec whenever you run commands that depend on gems. This ensures that you're using the correct versions of the gems.
- **Be careful when updating gems:** Before running bundle update, make sure you have a backup of your application and that you understand the potential risks. Updating gems can sometimes break your application if the updated gems introduce compatibility issues.

My "Gem Disaster" Story: I once accidentally updated a gem without thoroughly testing the changes. It broke a critical part of my application, and it took me hours to figure out what was going on. From that day forward, I always made sure to back up my application and test all changes thoroughly before updating gems.

Key Takeaways:

- The Gemfile lists all the gem dependencies for your application.
- Bundler manages your application's gem dependencies, ensuring that it uses the correct versions of all the necessary libraries.
- The Gemfile.lock file records the exact versions of all the gems that were installed.
- Always use Bundler to manage your gem dependencies.
- Commit the Gemfile.lock file to your version control system.

Understanding the Gemfile and Bundler is essential for managing your application's dependencies and ensuring that it runs smoothly. Follow the best practices outlined above, and you'll be well-prepared to handle any dependency-related challenges.

4.4 Starting the Rails Server: Bringing Your App to Life!

You've set up your environment, created your first Rails project, and explored the project structure. Now, it's time to bring your application to life by starting the Rails server! This is where the magic happens, and you'll finally see your code running in a web browser.

Think of the Rails server as the engine that powers your application. It listens for incoming requests from web browsers, processes those requests, and sends back responses that are displayed to the user.

The rails server Command: A Detailed Look

The command to start the Rails server is, unsurprisingly, rails server. But let's break down the details:

1. **Open Your Terminal:** Navigate to the root directory of your Rails application. This is the directory that contains the Gemfile, Rakefile, and other key files and directories.
2. **Run the Command:** Type the following command and press Enter:
3.   `rails server`

You can also use the shorthand command:

    `rails s`

IGNORE_WHEN_COPYING_START

content_copy download

Use code with caution.Bash

IGNORE_WHEN_COPYING_END

What Happens When You Run rails server?

When you run the rails server command, several things happen behind the scenes:

- **Rails boots up:** The Rails application is loaded and initialized. This involves loading the configuration files, connecting to the database, and loading all the necessary gems and code.
- **A web server starts:** A web server (usually Puma or WEBrick) is started. This server listens for incoming requests on a specific port (by default, port 3000).
- **The server listens for requests:** The server waits for requests from web browsers. When a request is received, Rails processes it and generates a response.
- **The response is sent to the browser:** The server sends the response back to the browser, which displays the content to the user.

Viewing Your Application in the Browser

Once the Rails server is running, you can view your application in a web browser by navigating to the following URL:

```
http://localhost:3000
```

- **localhost:** This refers to your local machine.
- **3000:** This is the port number that the Rails server is listening on. You can change the port number by specifying the -p option when starting the server (e.g., rails server -p 4000).

If everything is working correctly, you should see the default Rails welcome page. Congratulations! You've successfully started the Rails server and viewed your application in a web browser.

Customizing the Server (Optional)

The rails server command provides several options for customizing its behavior:

- -p <port>: Specifies the port number to listen on (e.g., rails server -p 4000).
- -b <bind>: Specifies the IP address to bind to (e.g., rails server -b 0.0.0.0). This is useful for accessing the server from other devices on your network.
- -e <environment>: Specifies the environment to run the server in (e.g., rails server -e production). By default, the server runs in the development environment.

Common Issues and Troubleshooting

- **"Address already in use":** If you get an "Address already in use" error, it means that another application is already listening on port 3000. You can either stop the other application or use the -p option to start the Rails server on a different port.
- **"Could not find gem...":** This error usually indicates a dependency issue. Make sure you've run bundle install to install all the required gems.
- **Blank page or error message:** If you see a blank page or an error message, check the server logs in your terminal for more information. The logs often provide clues about what went wrong.

- **Server not responding:** If the server is not responding, make sure it's running correctly and that you've entered the correct URL in your browser.

My "First Server" Experience: I remember the excitement of starting the Rails server for the first time and seeing the default welcome page. It was a tangible sign that I was actually building something real. It was also a bit intimidating, as I didn't understand what was happening behind the scenes. But as I learned more about Rails, the server became less of a black box and more of a familiar friend.

Key Takeaways:

- The rails server (or rails s) command starts the Rails server.
- The server listens for incoming requests on port 3000 by default.
- You can view your application in a web browser by navigating to http://localhost:3000.
- The server logs in your terminal provide valuable information for debugging.

Starting the Rails server is a crucial step in the web development process. It allows you to see your code in action and interact with your application in a web browser. So, go ahead, start the server, and enjoy the fruits of your labor!

4.5 Hello, World!: Your First Steps with MVC in Rails

You've started the Rails server and.application.routes.draw do
root 'welcome#index' #Maps root of application to controller "welcome" and action "index"
end
```

```
     This code defines a route that maps the root URL (`/`)
to the `index` action of the `WelcomeController`. The seen
the default welcome page. Now, it's time to create something
custom - a classic "Hello, World!" application! This will
give you a fundamental `root` method is a special method that
defines the root URL of your application.
```

1. **Restart the Rails Server:** After making changes to the routes, you need to restart the Rails server so that it picks up the changes.
```

2. **View the "Hello, World!" Page:** Open your web browser and navigate to http://localhost:3000. You should see the "Hello, world!" message displayed on the page.

Congratulations! You've successfully created a basic route, controller, and view in Rails. You've taken your first steps in understanding the MVC architecture.

Understanding the Flow:

Here's how the request flows through the MVC components:

1. **The browser sends a request to the root URL (/).**
2. **The Rails router matches the URL to the root 'welcome#index' route.**
3. **The router dis understanding of the Model-View-Controller (MVC) architecture, which is the cornerstone of Rails development.

Think of this as your first building project. You'll create a basic structure (the route), a processing unit (the controller), and a display area (the view). Together, they'll work to deliver the simple message "Hello, World!" to the user.

Understanding MVC (Briefly)

Before we dive into the code, let's briefly review the MVC architecture:

- **Model:** Represents the data and business logic of your application.
- **View:** Responsible for rendering the user interface.
- **Controller:** Handles user requests, interacts with the models, and selects the appropriate view to render.

Step by Step: Creating thepatches the request to the index action of the WelcomeController.
4. **The index action sets the @message instance variable to "Hello, world!".**
5. **The index action renders the `app/views/welcome/index.html.erb "Hello, World!" Application**

Let's create a WelcomeController with an index action that displays the message "Hello, World!".

1. **Generate the Controller (using the command line!):** Open your terminal and navigate to your Rails application directory. Run the following command to` view.**
2. **The view displays the value of the @message instance variable.**
3. **The server sends the generated HTML back to the browser.**
4. **The browser displays the "Hello, world!" message to the user.**

Digging Deeper

- ** generate a controller called welcome:

```
rails generate controller welcome index
```

This command will create several files:

- app/controllers/welcome_controller.rb: The controller file.
- `app/views/welcome/index.html.Controllers as Orchestrators:** Think of controllers as conductors of an orchestra. They direct the flow of data, tell models what to do, and decide which views to render. They should be lean and focused, avoiding complex logic.
- **Views as Presenters:** Views are responsible for presenting data in a user-erb`: The view file.
  - app/helpers/welcome_helper.rb: A helper file for the controller (we won't use this right now).
  - config/routes.rb: This file will be modified to create the route.
  - test/controllers/welcome_controller_test.rb: The test file (we will discuss this later).
  - app/assets/stylesheets/welcome.scss: The styling file.

1. **Modify the Controller:** Open the app/controllers/welcome_controller.rb file and add the following code:

```
    class WelcomeController < ApplicationController
  def index
    @message = "Hello, world!" #Define a method called index
and assign "Hello, world!" to the instance variable @message
  end
end
```

This code defines a controller called `friendly format. They should be kept as simple as possible, focusing on presentation rather than logic.

- **Models as Data Experts:** Models are responsible for managing data and interacting with the database. They should encapsulate the business logic related to your data.

My "Aha" Moment with MVC: It took me a while to truly grasp the separation of concerns that MVC promotes. But once I understood how each component had a specific role to play, my code became much more organized and maintainable. It was like having a clear blueprint for building web applications.

Key Takeaways:

- Controllers handle user requests and coordinate between models and views.
- Views render the user interface.
- Routes map URLs to controller actions.
- The MVC architecture promotes a clear separation of concerns, making your code more organized and maintainable.

Creating a basic route, controller, and view is a fundamental skill for any Rails developer. Practice these steps, experiment with different variations, and you'll be well on your way to mastering the art of web development with Rails.

Chapter 5: The Model-View-Controller (MVC) Architecture: Organizing Your Rails World

You've created your first Rails application, and you've seen a glimpse of how the different components work together. Now, let's delve deeper into the underlying structure that organizes everything: the Model-View-Controller (MVC) architecture.

Think of MVC as the architectural blueprint for your Rails application. It provides a clear and consistent way to separate concerns, making your code more organized, maintainable, and testable. Mastering MVC is essential for building complex and scalable Rails applications.

5.1 Deconstructing MVC: The Core Trio of Web Development

You've heard the term "MVC" thrown around, but what does it *really* mean? MVC, or Model-View-Controller, is an architectural pattern that divides an application into three interconnected parts, each with a specific responsibility. It is key to understanding not only Rails but many web frameworks in other languages as well. Think of MVC as a set of guidelines for organizing your code and ensuring that different parts of your application are well-separated and independent.

Mastering MVC is like learning the rules of the road. It gives you a framework for navigating the complexities of web development and building robust and maintainable applications. Let's explore each component in detail.

The Model: The Data Expert

The Model represents the data and business logic of your application. It's responsible for interacting with the database, enforcing data integrity rules, and performing any necessary calculations or transformations on the data.

Think of the Model as the warehouse and processing center for your data. It's where all the raw materials (data) are stored, and where they are transformed into finished products (meaningful information).

Key responsibilities of the Model:

- **Data storage and retrieval:** Interacting with the database to retrieve, create, update, and delete data.
- **Data validation:** Ensuring that the data is valid and consistent before it's stored in the database.
- **Business logic:** Implementing the rules and logic that govern your data.

Example: In a blog application, the Article model would be responsible for storing and retrieving article data, validating the title and content, and performing any necessary transformations on the data (e.g., converting Markdown to HTML).

The Model is usually connected to a single table on your database, and will be able to do CRUD actions on them.

The View: The Presentation Specialist

The View is responsible for rendering the user interface. It takes the data from the Model and displays it to the user in a visually appealing and understandable format.

Think of the View as the art gallery. It takes the raw materials (data) and transforms them into an engaging and informative display.

Key responsibilities of the View:

- **Data presentation:** Displaying data from the Model to the user.
- **User interface:** Generating the HTML, CSS, and JavaScript code that creates the user interface.
- **Minimal logic:** The View should contain minimal logic. It should primarily focus on presentation and avoid complex calculations or data manipulations.

Example: In a blog application, the Article view would be responsible for displaying the title, content, and author of an article. It would use HTML, CSS, and JavaScript to create a visually appealing and user-friendly interface.

The Controller: The Traffic Director

The Controller acts as an intermediary between the user, the Models, and the Views. It handles user requests, interacts with the Models to retrieve or modify data, and then selects the appropriate View to render the results to the user.

Think of the Controller as the air traffic controller. It directs the flow of data and ensures that everything gets to its destination safely and efficiently.

Key responsibilities of the Controller:

- **Request handling:** Receiving and processing user requests.
- **Model interaction:** Interacting with the Models to retrieve or modify data.
- **View selection:** Selecting the appropriate View to render the results to the user.
- **Data preparation:** Preparing the data for the View.

Example: In a blog application, the ArticlesController would be responsible for handling requests to create, view, update, and delete articles. It would interact with the Article model to perform these actions, and then select the appropriate view to display the results to the user.

Why This Separation Matters

You may be thinking this is all arbitrary and complicated. However, splitting into these three components makes the application a lot easier to maintain. For instance, the design of the application (how it looks) is separated from the data and the business logic. So if you ever decide to re-design the application you will not have to modify the other parts.

Analogy Time: Imagine you are building a car. The Model is the Engine, Axle, etc (How it works), the View is the seats, steering wheel and dashboard (How it looks), the Controller is the driver (taking action and instructing what the Model and View needs to do).

My "MVC Revelation" Moment: For a long time, I was just writing code without thinking about the underlying architecture. It worked, but it was messy and difficult to maintain. Once I started using MVC, my code became much more organized and maintainable. It was like having a clear roadmap for building applications.

Key Takeaways:

- MVC is an architectural pattern that divides an application into three interconnected parts: Model, View, and Controller.
- The Model represents the data and business logic of your application.
- The View is responsible for rendering the user interface.
- The Controller acts as an intermediary between the user, the Models, and the Views.
- MVC promotes a clear separation of concerns, making your code more organized, maintainable, and testable.

Understanding the core components of MVC is essential for building robust and scalable Rails applications. Take the time to grasp these concepts, and you'll be well-prepared for your web development journey.

5.2 How Rails Implements MVC: The "Rails Magic" Explained

You now understand the basic principles of MVC. But how does Rails *actually* implement this pattern? What are the specific conventions and tools that Rails provides to make MVC development easier? That's what we'll explore in this section.

Think of Rails as a conductor leading an orchestra (your application). Each section is an instrument and the result when combining the elements together is a harmonious song. It provides a framework for organizing your code, handling requests, interacting with the database, and rendering views, all while adhering to the MVC principles.

Models in Rails: Active Record to the Rescue

In Rails, models are typically Ruby classes that inherit from ApplicationRecord. They are located in the app/models/ directory. Rails models use Active Record, an ORM (Object-Relational Mapping) that simplifies database interactions.

Active Record provides a set of methods for performing CRUD (Create, Read, Update, Delete) operations on your database tables. It allows you to interact with the database using Ruby code, rather than writing SQL queries directly.

Example: app/models/article.rb

```
    class Article < ApplicationRecord #All models inheret
from ApplicationRecord
  validates :title, presence: true, length: { minimum: 5 }
#Validates to make sure it has a title that is present with a
minimum of 5 chars
end
```

Key points:

- class Article < ApplicationRecord: This defines an Article model that inherits from ApplicationRecord. All models in Rails inherit from ApplicationRecord.
- validates :title, presence: true, length: { minimum: 5 }: This adds a validation to ensure that the title attribute is present and has a minimum length of 5 characters. Validations help ensure data integrity.
- Database table name is automatically inferred as articles based on the model name.
- You can now perform CRUD operations on the articles table using methods like Article.all, Article.find, Article.new, article.save, and article.destroy.

Views in Rails: ERB Templates and View Helpers

Views are typically ERB (Embedded Ruby) templates located in the app/views/ directory. They contain HTML with embedded Ruby code to dynamically generate content.

Rails provides view helpers to simplify common view tasks, such as generating forms, creating links, and formatting data. View helpers are methods that are available in your views and can be used to generate HTML code.

Example: app/views/articles/index.html.erb

```
    <h1>Listing articles</h1>

<table>
  <thead>
    <tr>
      <th>Title</th>
      <th>Text</th>
      <th colspan="3"></th>
    </tr>
```

```
  </thead>

  <tbody>
    <% @articles.each do |article| %>
      <tr>
        <td><%= article.title %></td>
        <td><%= article.text %></td>
        <td><%= link_to 'Show', article_path(article) %></td>
        <td><%= link_to 'Edit', edit_article_path(article)
%></td>
        <td><%= link_to 'Destroy', article_path(article),
                    method: :delete,
                    data: { confirm: 'Are you sure?' }
%></td>
      </tr>
    <% end %>
  </tbody>
</table>

<%= link_to 'New article', new_article_path %>
```

Key points:

- <h1>Listing articles</h1>: This is a standard HTML heading.
- <% @articles.each do |article| %>: This is a Ruby loop that iterates over the @articles instance variable, which is set by the controller.
- <%= article.title %>: This displays the value of the title attribute of the article object.
- <%= link_to 'Show', article_path(article) %>: This uses the link_to helper to generate a link to the show action for the specified article. Rails automatically generates the URL based on the route configuration. View helpers are useful because they provide a consistent and secure way to generate HTML code.
- <%= link_to 'New article', new_article_path %>: Similarly, this line generates a link to create a new article

Controllers in Rails: Actions and Filters

Controllers are Ruby classes that inherit from ApplicationController. They are located in the app/controllers/ directory. Rails controllers use actions (methods) to handle specific requests.

Controllers also use filters (also known as callbacks) to perform actions before, after, or around specific actions. Filters can be used for tasks such as authentication, authorization, and data preparation.

Example: app/controllers/articles_controller.rb

```ruby
class ArticlesController < ApplicationController
#Inherits from ApplicationController
  before_action :set_article, only: [:show, :edit, :update,
:destroy] #Runs set_article method for show, edit, update,
destroy actions

  def index #Action is invoked by the route to the action
    @articles = Article.all #Retrieves all articles from the
database
  end

  def show #action is invoked by the route to the action

  end

  private
    def set_article #This can only be called inside the
controller.
      @article = Article.find(params[:id])
    end
end
```

Key points:

- class ArticlesController < ApplicationController: This defines an ArticlesController that inherits from ApplicationController.
- before_action :set_article, only: [:show, :edit, :update, :destroy]: This is a filter that calls the set_article method before the show, edit, update, and destroy actions. This ensures that the @article instance variable is always set before these actions are executed.

Action Controller Parameters

When passing properties that can be set to the Models for either editing or creating a Model, Rails introduced a way to sanitize and authorize attributes called "strong parameters." This prevents users from manipulating attributes that they should not be able to set.

```ruby
def create
@article = Article.new(article_params)

if @article.save
  redirect_to @article
else
```

```
      render :new
    end
  end

  private
  def article_params
    params.require(:article).permit(:title, :text)
  end
```

Key points:

- params.require(:article) Specifies the key that needs to be present in the params hash (the data the user sent in to edit or create). If article does not exist, it will throw an error.
- .permit(:title, :text) Specifies which attributes that the user is authorized to set on the Article

Routes: Mapping URLs to Controller Actions

Rails uses a routing system to map URLs to controller actions. The routes are defined in the config/routes.rb file.

Example: config/routes.rb

```
Rails.application.routes.draw do
  resources :articles #This autogenerates routes for CRUD
actions.
end
```

- resources :articles: This line generates a set of routes for the ArticlesController, including routes for listing, creating, viewing, updating, and deleting articles.
- For instance, going to the route articles/new will call the action new on the Article controller, and the system will look for app/views/articles/new.html.erb

The "Rails Magic" Unveiled

Rails implements the MVC pattern by providing a set of conventions and tools that make it easy to create well-organized and maintainable applications. Rails automatically infers the names of database tables, models, controllers, and views based on conventions. It also provides powerful tools like Active Record and view helpers to simplify common tasks.

My "Aha" Moment with Rails Conventions: I remember the first time I used a Rails generator to create a model, controller, and views. I was amazed at how quickly it generated all the necessary files and code. It was like the framework was reading my mind and doing all the work for me! This was the beauty of "convention over configuration," and when it clicked.

Key Takeaways:

- Rails implements the MVC pattern using models that inherit from ApplicationRecord, views that are ERB templates, and controllers that inherit from ApplicationController.
- Active Record simplifies database interactions.
- View helpers simplify common view tasks.
- Routes map URLs to controller actions.
- Rails uses conventions to infer the names of database tables, models, controllers, and views.

Understanding how Rails implements the MVC pattern is essential for building well-structured and maintainable applications. By following the Rails conventions, you can focus on the unique aspects of your application, rather than getting bogged down in boilerplate code.

5.3 Data Flow in Rails: Tracing the Journey of a Web Request

You've grasped the core concepts of MVC and how Rails implements them. Now, let's trace the journey of a web request through your Rails application, from the moment a user clicks a link or submits a form to the moment they see the results in their browser. Understanding this data flow is crucial for debugging, optimizing performance, and building secure and scalable applications.

Think of the data flow as the circulatory system of your application. It's the path that data takes as it travels through the different components, delivering information where it needs to go.

The Request-Response Cycle: A Step-by-Step Guide

Here's a detailed breakdown of the data flow in a typical Rails application:

1. **The User Makes a Request:** It all starts with the user. They might type a URL into their browser's address bar, click a link, submit a form, or perform some other action that triggers a request.
   - **Example:** The user clicks a link to view an article with ID 5. This sends a request to the URL articles/5.
2. **The Web Server Receives the Request:** The web server (e.g., Puma) receives the request and passes it on to the Rails application.
3. **The Router Maps the URL to a Controller Action:** The Rails router, defined in config/routes.rb, examines the URL and determines which controller action should handle the request.
   - **Example:** The router matches the URL articles/5 to the route defined by resources :articles, which maps it to the show action of the ArticlesController.
4. **The Controller Receives the Request:** The controller receives the request and performs the necessary actions to handle it.
   - **Example:** The ArticlesController's show action is called.
5. **The Controller Interacts with the Model:** The controller interacts with the model (typically using Active Record) to retrieve or modify data.
   - **Example:** The show action uses Article.find(5) to retrieve the article with ID 5 from the database.
6. **The Model Interacts with the Database:** The model (using Active Record) interacts with the database to retrieve or modify the data. This may involve executing SQL queries.
   - **Example:** Active Record generates a SQL SELECT query to retrieve the article with ID 5 from the articles table.
7. **The Database Returns the Data:** The database returns the data to the model.
   - **Example:** The database returns the row from the articles table with ID 5.
8. **The Model Passes the Data to the Controller:** The model passes the data back to the controller.
   - **Example:** The Article.find(5) method returns an Article object representing the article with ID 5.
9. **The Controller Prepares Data for the View:** The controller may perform additional processing on the data before passing it to the view. This might involve formatting the data, performing calculations, or creating additional data structures.
   - **Example:** The show action assigns the @article instance variable, which will be available in the view.

10. **The Controller Selects and Renders a View:** The controller selects the appropriate view to render the results to the user. This is typically based on the request format (e.g., HTML, JSON) and the type of data being displayed. The controller then renders the view, passing it any necessary data.
    o **Example:** The show action renders the app/views/articles/show.html.erb view, passing it the @article instance variable.
11. **The View Generates the HTML:** The view uses ERB (Embedded Ruby) to generate the HTML code that will be displayed in the browser. The view embeds Ruby code to dynamically display data from the model and generate dynamic HTML elements.
    o **Example:** The app/views/articles/show.html.erb view uses <%= @article.title %> to display the title of the article.
12. **The Server Sends the Response to the Browser:** The Rails server sends the generated HTML back to the browser as the response to the original request.
13. **The Browser Renders the HTML:** The browser receives the HTML and renders it, displaying the content to the user.
    o **Example:** The browser displays the title, content, and author of the article.

A Visual Summary

To summarize, the journey is: User > Router > Controller > Model > Database > Model > Controller > View > User

Debugging Data Flow

Understanding the data flow is crucial for debugging Rails applications. When you encounter an error, you can use the data flow to trace the problem back to its source.

Troubleshooting Tips

- Start by examining the server logs in your terminal. The logs often provide clues about what went wrong, such as routing errors, database errors, or view rendering errors.
- Use binding.pry (Pry gem) to pause the execution of your code at specific points and inspect the values of variables. This allows you to see exactly what's happening at each step of the data flow.

- Use the Rails console to interact with your models and the database. This allows you to test your database queries and ensure that the data is being retrieved and modified correctly.
- Use your browser's developer tools to inspect the HTML that is being generated by your views. This allows you to see if the data is being displayed correctly.

My "Data Flow" Epiphany: I remember struggling to debug a complex Rails application. I kept making changes to the code, but nothing seemed to fix the problem. Finally, I realized that I needed to step back and understand the data flow. Once I understood how the data was traveling through the application, I was able to quickly identify the source of the error and fix it.

Key Takeaways:

- Understanding the data flow is crucial for debugging, optimizing performance, and building secure and scalable Rails applications.
- The data flow starts with the user making a request and ends with the browser displaying the content to the user.
- The Rails router, controller, model, and view each play a specific role in the data flow.
- Debugging tips for understanding the various parts when data gets held up.

By understanding the data flow in a Rails application, you'll gain a deeper appreciation for how the different components work together and be better equipped to build and maintain complex web applications.

Okay, let's craft an engaging and persuasive guide on the benefits of using the MVC architecture, designed to resonate with your beginner audience and solidify the value proposition of MVC.

5.4 Why Bother with MVC? The Payoff for Structure

You've spent the last few sections diving deep into the details of the Model-View-Controller (MVC) architecture. You might be thinking, "This seems like a lot of overhead! Is it *really* worth it?"

The answer is a resounding **yes!** While MVC may seem complex at first, it offers a multitude of benefits that will make your life as a web developer easier, more productive, and more enjoyable.

Think of MVC as an investment in the future of your application. It's a way to build a solid foundation that will support growth, maintainability, and collaboration.

Let's explore the key benefits of using MVC:

1. Separation of Concerns: Code Organization Bliss

This is the most fundamental benefit of MVC. By separating your application into distinct components (Model, View, and Controller), you create a clear separation of concerns. This means that each component has a specific responsibility and is independent of the other components.

- **Benefit:** Makes code easier to understand, maintain, and debug. You can focus on one component at a time without having to worry about the complexities of the other components.
- **Example:** If you need to change the way data is stored or retrieved, you can focus on the Model without having to modify the View or Controller.

2. Code Reusability: Write Once, Use Everywhere

MVC promotes code reusability. Models can be used by multiple controllers, and views can be used to display data from multiple models. This reduces code duplication and makes your application more efficient.

- **Benefit:** Saves time and effort. You can avoid writing the same code multiple times, and you can easily reuse existing components in new parts of your application.
- **Example:** You might have a User model that is used by multiple controllers to manage user accounts, profiles, and authentication. Similarly, a reusable "form" view can be used to create all kinds of forms to render user interfaces.

3. Testability: Confident Code

MVC makes it easier to test your application. You can test each component independently, ensuring that they are working correctly.

- **Benefit:** Increases the reliability of your application. You can catch bugs early in the development process, before they make it into production.

- **Example:** You can write unit tests for your models to ensure that they are correctly interacting with the database. You can also write integration tests to ensure that the controllers, models, and views are working together correctly.

4. Parallel Development: Teamwork Makes the Dream Work

MVC facilitates parallel development. Different developers can work on different components of the application simultaneously without interfering with each other's work.

- **Benefit:** Speeds up the development process. You can divide the work among multiple developers, allowing you to deliver features faster.
- **Example:** One developer can work on the models, another can work on the views, and a third can work on the controllers, all at the same time.

5. Maintainability: Future-Proofing Your Application

MVC makes your application easier to maintain over time. As your application grows and evolves, the clear separation of concerns makes it easier to add new features, modify existing features, and fix bugs.

- **Benefit:** Reduces the cost of maintaining your application. You can make changes to the code without having to worry about breaking other parts of the application.
- **Example:** If you need to change the database schema, you can do so without having to modify the views or controllers.

6. Scalability: Building for the Future

MVC makes it easier to scale your application to handle increasing traffic and data volumes. The modular structure of MVC allows you to optimize individual components without affecting the performance of other components.

- **Benefit:** Ensures that your application can handle growth. You can scale your application to handle more users and more data without having to rewrite the entire application.
- **Example:** You can optimize your database queries to improve performance without having to modify the views or controllers.

7. Code Organization: With the right file structure in a specific directory, it's very easy to locate code and make changes.

Analogy Time: Think of building a house. If you just start throwing materials together without a plan, you'll end up with a disorganized mess that's difficult to live in and even harder to expand or repair. MVC is like having a detailed blueprint that ensures every part of the house is well-organized and serves a specific purpose.

My "MVC Conversion" Story: I used to resist using MVC because it seemed like overkill for small projects. But as I started working on larger and more complex applications, I realized that MVC was essential for managing the complexity. It transformed my code from a tangled mess into a well-organized and maintainable system. I could quickly navigate and understand the code.

Key Takeaways:

- The benefits of using the MVC architecture far outweigh the initial learning curve.
- MVC promotes separation of concerns, code reusability, testability, parallel development, maintainability, and scalability.
- MVC is an investment in the future of your application.
- Once you embrace MVC, you'll never go back!

By understanding the benefits of MVC, you'll be more motivated to learn and apply this powerful architectural pattern in your Rails projects. It's a skill that will serve you well throughout your web development career. So, embrace MVC, and get ready to build amazing things!

Chapter 6: Models and Databases with PostgreSQL - Where Your Data Lives

You've mastered the basics of MVC and created your first Rails application. Now, let's dive into the heart of most web applications: the *database*. This is where you store and manage all the important information that powers your application, such as user accounts, product details, blog posts, and more.

In this chapter, we'll learn how to connect your Rails application to a PostgreSQL database, create models to represent your data, and perform common database operations.

6.1 Connecting Rails to PostgreSQL: Building the Foundation for Your Data

You've set the stage with models, and now it's time to hook them up to a real database! This is the first critical step to making your application dynamic and able to store and retrieve data. The database is where your application's persistent data lives. We'll use PostgreSQL, a powerful and reliable open-source database system, as our data store.

Think of this as laying the foundation for your application's data warehouse. A solid and well-configured foundation is essential for building a strong and scalable application.

The database.yml File: Your Connection Hub

Rails uses the database.yml file, located in the config/ directory, to store the database connection settings. This file contains the configuration settings for your application's database connection in various environments (development, test, and production). Think of this as your database settings central.

Configuration Steps:

1. **Open the config/database.yml file:** Use your code editor to open the config/database.yml file.

2. **Understanding the Structure:** You'll see a YAML file with sections for different environments: default, development, test, and production. The default section defines common settings that are inherited by the other environments.

```
    default: &default
  adapter: postgresql
  encoding: unicode
  pool: <%= ENV.fetch("RAILS_MAX_THREADS") { 5 } %>
  username: your_username #This is the username to connect to
your postgress database
  password: your_password #Password for your postgress user
  host: localhost #Host of the database. For production and
dedicated dbs this will change

development: # settings for development
  <<: *default #Uses the same settings as default unless
overridden
  database: my_first_app_development #Datase name for the dev
environment. You'll need to create this db.

test: #settings for testing
  <<: *default #Uses the same settings as default unless
overridden
  database: my_first_app_test #Datase name for the test
environment. You'll need to create this db.

production: #settings for production
  <<: *default #Uses the same settings as default unless
overridden
  database: my_first_app_production #Datase name for the
production environment. You'll need to create this db.
```

3. **Modify the database.yml File:** Edit the file to match your PostgreSQL database settings. The key settings are:
    o adapter: postgresql: Specifies the database adapter to use. Make sure this is set to postgresql.
    o encoding: unicode: Specifies the character encoding to use. Unicode is recommended for handling a wide range of characters.
    o pool: <%= ENV.fetch("RAILS_MAX_THREADS") { 5 } %>: Specifies the number of database connections to keep in the connection pool. The connection pool helps improve performance by reusing existing database connections.
    o username: your_username: Replace your_username with your PostgreSQL username. This is the username you use to

connect to your PostgreSQL database. If you're not sure what your username is, you can try using your operating system username.

- o password: your_password: Replace your_password with your PostgreSQL password. This is the password you use to connect to your PostgreSQL database.
- o host: localhost: Specifies the hostname of the database server. In most cases, you'll use localhost for local development. In a production environment, this would be the hostname or IP address of your database server.
- o database: my_first_app_development: Replace my_first_app_development with the name of your development database. This is the name of the PostgreSQL database that you want to use for your development environment. Repeat this process for the test and production databases.

Important Security Note: Never store your database password directly in the database.yml file in a production environment. Instead, use environment variables to store sensitive information.

Creating the Databases:

Now that you've configured the database settings, you need to create the databases in PostgreSQL. You can do this using the rails db:create command:

```
rails db:create
```

This command will create the development, test, and production databases based on the settings in your database.yml file.

Troubleshooting: If you get errors, be sure to specify the right connection details. If that doesn't work you may need to install the gem pg if it's not set

Verifying the Connection

After creating the databases, it's a good idea to verify that the connection is working correctly. You can do this by running the following command:

```
rails db:migrate
```

This command will run any pending database migrations. Migrations are Ruby files that define changes to your database schema. Running this command will create the basic tables, and you can check the PostgreSQL logs to see if any errors were encountered.

Digging Deeper: Understanding the ENV Variable

You may notice that the pool setting in database.yml uses the ENV.fetch("RAILS_MAX_THREADS") syntax. This is a way to read environment variables. Environment variables are variables that are set outside of your application code. They are commonly used to store configuration settings that vary between environments.

My Connection Story: Setting up the database connection for the first time felt like a rite of passage. Getting those credentials right and seeing the confirmation that the database was connected was a huge milestone. A mistake many beginners make is to overlook what username and password the postgres database is using, so make sure to check that!

Key Takeaways:

- The database.yml file configures the database connection settings for your Rails application.
- You need to specify the database adapter, username, password, host, and database name in the database.yml file.
- You should create separate databases for development, test, and production environments.
- You can use the rails db:create command to create the databases.
- It's important to verify the connection after configuring the database settings.

Connecting your Rails application to a PostgreSQL database is a fundamental step in building dynamic and data-driven web applications. By following these steps, you'll be well-prepared to start building models, migrations, and other database-related code.

6.2 Creating Models with Migrations: Sculpting Your Data Landscape

You've successfully connected your Rails application to a PostgreSQL database. Now, it's time to define the structure of your data using *models* and *migrations*.

Think of models as the blueprints for your data. They define the attributes (columns) and relationships that characterize your data. Migrations, on the other hand, are the tools you use to create and modify the database schema based on those models. It's through migrations that you sculpt the landscape of your data.

What are Rails Migrations?

Migrations are Ruby files that define changes to your database schema. They provide a controlled and repeatable way to create, modify, and delete tables, columns, and indexes. Migrations are essential for managing the evolution of your database structure over time.

Why Use Migrations?

- **Version Control for Your Database:** Migrations are stored in your version control system (e.g., Git), allowing you to track changes to your database schema over time.
- **Repeatable Database Setup:** You can easily recreate your database schema on different environments (development, test, production) by running the migrations.
- **Collaborative Development:** Migrations allow multiple developers to work on the same database schema without conflicts.

The rails generate model Command: Your Starting Point

The easiest way to create a model and migration is to use the rails generate model command. This command generates both the model file (app/models/) and the migration file (db/migrate/).

Example: Let's create a model called Article with two attributes: title (string) and text (text).

```
rails generate model Article title:string text:text
```

Let's break down this command:

- rails generate model: This tells Rails to generate a model and migration.
- Article: This is the name of the model.
- title:string: This specifies an attribute called title with a data type of string.
- text:text: This specifies an attribute called text with a data type of text.

Rails will then create the Model and migration files. If you don't specify the datatypes, then the database will not automatically set them. If you've already created the Model, it will be skipped and only create the migration file.

Understanding the Migration File

The rails generate model command creates a migration file in the db/migrate/ directory. The migration file has a timestamped name (e.g., 20231027123456_create_articles.rb).

Let's take a look at the contents of the migration file:

```
      class CreateArticles < ActiveRecord::Migration[7.0]
#Specifies this as a migration
  def change #runs with migrate
    create_table :articles do |t|   #Creates a database table
called articles
      t.string :title #creates a string column called title
      t.text :text #creates a text column called text

      t.timestamps #creates created_at and updated_at column
to store time stamps
    end
  end
end
```

Key points:

- class CreateArticles < ActiveRecord::Migration[7.0]: This defines a migration class called CreateArticles that inherits from ActiveRecord::Migration. The [7.0] specifies the Rails version.
- def change: This defines the change method, which contains the code to create the articles table.
- create_table :articles do |t| ... end: This creates a table called articles. The t object is a table definition object that provides methods for creating columns.
- t.string :title: This creates a column called title with a data type of string.
- t.text :text: This creates a column called text with a data type of text.
- t.timestamps: This creates two columns called created_at and updated_at, which store the timestamps of when the record was created and last updated.

Running the Migration

To apply the changes defined in the migration, you need to run the migration using the rails db:migrate command:

```
rails db:migrate
```

This command will run all pending migrations, creating or modifying the database schema as needed.

Important Note: You should always run migrations in the correct order. Rails uses the timestamps in the migration filenames to determine the order in which to run them.

Understanding Rollbacks

Migrations also support rollbacks, which allow you to undo the changes made by a migration. This is useful if you need to revert to a previous version of your database schema.

To rollback the last migration, use the rails db:rollback command:

```
rails db:rollback
```

You can also rollback multiple migrations by specifying the number of migrations to rollback:

```
rails db:rollback STEP=3
```

Data Types

Rails supports a variety of data types for model attributes:

- string: For short text (e.g., names, titles)
- text: For longer text (e.g., article content)
- integer: For whole numbers
- float: For floating-point numbers
- decimal: For high-precision decimal numbers (e.g., currency)
- boolean: For true/false values
- date: For dates
- datetime: For dates and times
- timestamp: For timestamps

My "Migration Mishap" Story: I once accidentally ran a migration in the production environment without backing up the database first. It completely messed up the database schema, and it took me hours to restore the data. I learned the hard way that it's crucial to back up your database before running any migrations in production.

Key Takeaways:

- Models represent the data in your application.
- Migrations are used to create and modify the database schema based on your models.
- The rails generate model command generates both the model file and the migration file.
- The rails db:migrate command runs all pending migrations.
- Migrations support rollbacks, which allow you to undo the changes made by a migration.

Creating models with migrations is a fundamental skill for any Rails developer. By mastering these concepts, you'll be able to define the structure of your data and manage the evolution of your database schema over time.

6.3 Defining Model Attributes and Data Types: Sculpting Your Data Landscape

You've created your first model and migration! Now it's time to understand how to precisely define the *attributes* of your model. Attributes, in essence, are the columns in your database table, and they represent the characteristics or properties of the data you're storing. Furthermore, you'll learn to specify the *data types* for those attributes, which dictate what kind of information they can hold.

Think of defining attributes and data types as carefully selecting the right tools and materials for building a sculpture. You need to choose the right clay, chisel, and other instruments to achieve your desired result.

Adding Attributes to a Model

When you generate a model using rails generate model, you can specify the attributes and their data types directly in the command:

```
rails generate model Product name:string
description:text price:decimal{10,2} in_stock:boolean
```

This command will generate a model called Product with the following attributes:

- name: A string attribute to store the name of the product.
- description: A text attribute to store the description of the product.
- price: A decimal attribute to store the price of the product. The {10,2} part specifies that the decimal has a total of 10 digits, with 2 digits after the decimal point (e.g., 12345678.90).
- in_stock: A boolean attribute to store whether the product is in stock.

This will create a timestamped migration file inside the directory db/migrate

Manual Migration Creation and Editing

In many cases, you may need to add or modify attributes after you've already created the model. You can do this by creating a new migration file using the rails generate migration command:

```
rails generate migration AddAttributesToProducts
category:string weight:float
```

This will generate a migration file named something like db/migrate/20231027123456_add_attributes_to_products.rb. Open this file and modify it to add the new attributes:

```
class AddAttributesToProducts <
ActiveRecord::Migration[7.0]
  def change
    add_column :products, :category, :string #Add column
category of type string
    add_column :products, :weight, :float #Add column
category of type float
  end
end
```

Key points:

- add_column :products, :category, :string: This adds a column called category to the products table with a data type of string.
- add_column :products, :weight, :float: This adds a column called weight to the products table with a data type of float.

When you run rails db:migrate, these changes will be applied to the database.

Common Data Types

Rails supports a wide range of data types for model attributes. Here are some of the most commonly used ones:

- string: For short text (e.g., names, titles, email addresses)
- text: For longer text (e.g., descriptions, article content)
- integer: For whole numbers
- bigint: For even larger whole numbers
- float: For floating-point numbers
- decimal: For high-precision decimal numbers (e.g., currency)
- boolean: For true/false values
- date: For dates
- datetime: For dates and times
- timestamp: For timestamps

- references: For creating associations between models (we'll cover this in a later chapter)
- json: For json data structures

Choosing the Right Data Type

Choosing the right data type for your attributes is crucial for data integrity, storage efficiency, and performance. Consider the following factors when selecting a data type:

- **The type of data:** What kind of information will the attribute store?
- **The size of the data:** How much storage space will the attribute require?
- **The precision of the data:** How much precision is required for numerical values?
- **The performance implications:** Which data type will provide the best performance for queries and other database operations?

My "Data Type Disaster" Story: I once used the wrong data type for a price attribute, using a float instead of a decimal. This led to rounding errors that caused significant discrepancies in financial calculations. I learned that choosing the right data type is crucial for maintaining the accuracy of your data.

Key Takeaways:

- Model attributes represent the characteristics or properties of your data.
- Data types specify the kind of information an attribute can hold.
- The rails generate model and rails generate migration commands are used to create models and migrations.
- Choosing the right data type is crucial for data integrity, storage efficiency, and performance.

By understanding how to define model attributes and data types, you'll be able to create well-structured and efficient data models for your Rails applications. This is a fundamental skill for any Rails developer, and it will serve you well as you build more complex applications.

6.4 CRUD Operations via the Rails Console: Your Data Command Center

You've defined your models and created your database tables. Now it's time to learn how to interact with your data using the Rails console. The Rails console is a powerful command-line tool that allows you to execute Ruby code within the context of your Rails application. It's an invaluable tool for testing your models, querying your database, and performing various data manipulation tasks.

CRUD stands for **Create, Read, Update, and Delete**, which are the four basic operations that can be performed on persistent data. Mastering CRUD operations is essential for building dynamic web applications that can interact with a database.

Think of the Rails console as your data command center. It gives you direct access to your application's models and database, allowing you to perform operations with precision and control.

Launching the Rails Console

To start the Rails console, open your terminal, navigate to your Rails application directory, and run the following command:

```
rails console
```

You can also use the shorthand command:

```
rails c
```

This will launch the Rails console and display a prompt that looks something like this:

```
Loading development environment (Rails 7.0.0)
irb(main):001:0>
```

You are now ready to interact with your models and database.

The "C" in CRUD: Create - Adding New Data

To create a new record in your database, you can use the new and save methods of your model.

Example: Let's create a new Article record:

```
article = Article.new(title: "My First Article", text:
"This is the content of my first article.")
article.save
```

Let's break down this code:

- Article.new(...): This creates a new Article object in memory. It does *not* yet save the object to the database.
- title: "My First Article", text: "This is the content of my first article.": These are the attributes that we're setting for the new Article object.
- article.save: This saves the Article object to the database. If the save is successful, it returns true. If there are validation errors, it returns false.

You can also create and save a new record in a single step using the create method:

```
article = Article.create(title: "My Second Article",
text: "This is the content of my second article.")
```

The "R" in CRUD: Read - Retrieving Data

To retrieve data from your database, you can use the find, all, and where methods of your model.

- find(id): Retrieves a single record with the specified ID.

```
article = Article.find(1) # Find the article with ID 1
puts article.title       # Display the title
puts article.text        # Display the text
```

- all: Retrieves all records from the table.

```
articles = Article.all #Retrieves all articles
```

```
articles.each do |article| #Iterates through each article
  puts article.title #Prints the title of each article
end
```

- where(conditions): Retrieves records that match the specified conditions.

```
    articles = Article.where(title: "My First Article")
articles.each do |article|
  puts article.text
end
```

The "U" in CRUD: Update - Modifying Existing Data

To update an existing record in your database, you can use the find method to retrieve the record, modify its attributes, and then use the save method to persist the changes.

```
    article = Article.find(1) # find the article
article.title = "My Updated Article" #Sets a new title
article.save # saves the change
```

You can also update multiple attributes at once using the update method:

```
    article = Article.find(1)
article.update(title: "My Updated Title", text: "This is the
updated content.")
```

The "D" in CRUD: Delete - Removing Data

To delete a record from your database, you can use the find method to retrieve the record and then use the destroy method to delete it.

```
    article = Article.find(1)
article.destroy
```

You can also delete multiple records at once using the destroy_all method with certain conditions:

```
    Article.destroy_all(title: "My First Article")
```

Important Note: Be careful when using the destroy_all method, as it will permanently delete all records that match the specified conditions.

Putting It All Together

Let's combine all the CRUD operations into a single example:

```
    # Create
article = Article.create(title: "My New Article", text: "This
is the content.")

# Read
article = Article.find(article.id)
puts article.title

# Update
article.update(title: "My Updated Article")

# Delete
article.destroy
```

My "Console Power" Story: I remember the first time I used the Rails console to interact with a database. It felt like unlocking a secret door into my application. I could quickly test my models, query the database, and fix data issues without having to write any code. It became an indispensable tool in my development workflow.

Key Takeaways:

- The Rails console is a powerful tool for interacting with your models and database.
- CRUD stands for Create, Read, Update, and Delete, which are the four basic operations that can be performed on persistent data.
- The new, create, find, all, where, update, and destroy methods are used to perform CRUD operations.

By mastering CRUD operations in the Rails console, you'll gain a much deeper understanding of how your models interact with the database and be able to quickly test and debug your code.

6.5 Validations: Guarding Your Data with Ruby's Sentinels

You've learned how to create models, define attributes, and perform CRUD operations. Now, let's focus on ensuring that the data you're storing in your database is valid, consistent, and reliable. This is where *validations* come in.

Think of validations as security guards for your data. They stand watch at the entrance to your database, preventing invalid or malicious data from entering the system.

Why Use Validations?

- **Data Integrity:** Validations ensure that the data in your database is accurate and consistent.
- **Application Reliability:** By preventing invalid data from entering your application, validations help to improve its overall reliability.
- **Security:** Validations can help protect your application from security vulnerabilities, such as SQL injection and cross-site scripting (XSS).
- **User Experience:** Validations provide feedback to users when they enter invalid data, helping them correct their mistakes.

Declaring Validations in Your Model

Validations are declared in your model using the validates method. The validates method takes the name of the attribute to validate and a set of options that specify the validation rules.

Example: Let's add some validations to our Article model:

```
class Article < ApplicationRecord #This is a model
  validates :title, presence: true, length: { minimum: 5 }
#Requires the title to be present, and have a minimum of 5
characters
  validates :text, presence: true #requires the text to be
present
end
```

In this example, we've added two validations:

- validates :title, presence: true, length: { minimum: 5 }: This validation ensures that the title attribute is present (not nil or empty) and has a minimum length of 5 characters.

- validates :text, presence: true: This validation ensures that the text attribute is present.

Common Validation Options

Rails provides a wide range of validation options that you can use to customize your validation rules. Here are some of the most commonly used options:

- presence: true: Ensures that the attribute is present (not nil or empty).
- absence: true: Ensures that the attribute is absent (nil or empty).
- length: { minimum: x, maximum: y }: Specifies the minimum and maximum length of the attribute.
- numericality: true: Ensures that the attribute is a number.
- inclusion: { in: [...] }: Ensures that the attribute is included in a list of allowed values.
- exclusion: { in: [...] }: Ensures that the attribute is excluded from a list of disallowed values.
- uniqueness: true: Ensures that the attribute is unique across all records in the table.
- format: { with: /.../ }: Ensures that the attribute matches a regular expression.
- confirmation: true: Creates a virtual attribute (e.g., password_confirmation) that must match the original attribute (e.g., password).
- email: true: Requires that the field is a valid email address

Testing Your Validations

You can test your validations in the Rails console. Let's create a new Article object with invalid data and see what happens:

```
article = Article.new(title: "Hi", text: "") #Sets the title to be less than 5 chars, and text to be empty
article.save #Trys to save

article.errors.messages #Prints all of the errors in the article object
=> {:text=>["can't be blank"], :title=>["is too short (minimum is 5 characters)"]}
```

114

This code will create a new Article object with a title that is too short and a blank text attribute. When you call article.save, the validations will fail, and the save method will return false.

The article.errors.messages hash contains the validation errors for each attribute. You can use this hash to display error messages to the user.

Adding Custom Validation Methods

In some cases, you may need to create custom validation methods to implement more complex validation logic. You can do this by defining a method in your model and adding the validate method to your model.

```
    class Article < ApplicationRecord
  validate :title_must_be_unique_for_each_author #Adds a
custom validate method

  private #Private method to only be called from the class
itself
    def title_must_be_unique_for_each_author
      #Write code to ensure title is unque
    end
end
```

Displaying Validation Errors in Your Views

In your views, you can display validation errors to the user using the object.errors.full_messages.

Key Takeaways:

- Validations are essential for ensuring data integrity and application reliability.
- You can declare validations in your models using the validates method.
- Rails provides a wide range of validation options that you can use to customize your validation rules.
- You can test your validations in the Rails console.
- You can display validation errors in your views using the object.errors.full_messages method.

By mastering validations, you'll be able to build more robust and reliable Rails applications that protect your data and provide a better user experience.

Chapter 7: Views and Templates: Making Your Data Shine!

You've built your models and connected them to the database. Now, it's time to bring your data to life by creating views that display it to the user in a meaningful and engaging way.

Think of views as the stage on which your application's data performs. They're responsible for transforming raw data into a compelling and interactive experience for your users.

7.1 Crafting Views with ERB: Weaving Ruby into Your Web Pages

You've laid the foundation, now it's time to make your web application visually appealing and engaging. In Rails, the responsibility for rendering the user interface falls upon the *view*, and the primary tool for creating those views is **ERB (Embedded Ruby)**.

Think of ERB as your dynamic canvas, allowing you to weave Ruby code directly into your HTML to generate dynamic content, respond to user input, and create interactive web pages. It's what allows you to create dynamic web pages based on data from your models and controllers.

What is ERB?

ERB is a templating system for Ruby. It allows you to embed Ruby code into plain text files (usually HTML), which is then processed by the ERB engine to generate dynamic output. In Rails, views are typically written in ERB and have the .html.erb extension.

Why Use ERB?

- **Dynamic Content Generation:** ERB allows you to dynamically generate HTML content based on data from your models and controllers.
- **Code Reusability:** ERB supports layouts and partials, which allow you to create reusable UI components.

- **Separation of Concerns:** ERB helps you separate the presentation logic from the business logic, making your code more organized and maintainable.
- **Familiar Syntax:** If you know HTML and Ruby, you'll find ERB relatively easy to learn.

The Basics of ERB Syntax

ERB provides three main types of tags for embedding Ruby code into HTML:

1. **Output Tag (<%= ... %>):** Evaluates the Ruby code and inserts the result into the HTML output. This is used for displaying data. This is used to display a value from the code. For instance to display the title to the page.
2.
```
       <h1>Welcome, <%= @user.name %>!</h1>
```

   In this example, the <%= @user.name %> tag evaluates the Ruby code @user.name (which retrieves the name of the @user object) and inserts the result into the HTML output.

3. **Control Tag (<% ... %>):** Evaluates the Ruby code but does not insert the result into the HTML output. This is used for control flow, such as loops and conditional statements.
   This does not show any content on the page. Commonly used for loop and if statements.

```
    <% if @user.is_admin? %>
  <p>You have administrator privileges.</p>
<% end %>
```

   In this example, the <% if @user.is_admin? %> and <% end %> tags create a conditional statement that displays the "You have administrator privileges." message only if the @user object has the is_admin? method that returns true.

4. **Comment Tag (<# ... #>):** Comments out the Ruby code, so it's not executed or displayed in the output. For comments only, will not show up on the page or try to execute.

```
<# This code is commented out and will not be executed
#>
```

Creating Your First View

Let's create a simple view that displays a list of articles.

1. **Create a Controller:** First, you need a controller that sets up the data
   for the view. Create a file called app/controllers/articles_controller.rb
   with the following content:

```
    class ArticlesController < ApplicationController
  def index
    @articles = Article.all #Load all the articles from the
database
  end
end
```

2. **Create a Route:** Add a route to your config/routes.rb file that maps
   the /articles URL to the index action of the ArticlesController:

```
    Rails.application.routes.draw do
  get 'articles/index'
  resources :articles
  # other routes...
end
```

3. **Create a View:** Now, create the view file
   app/views/articles/index.html.erb with the following content:

```
    <h1>Listing Articles</h1>
<ul>
  <% @articles.each do |article| %> #For each article
    <li>
      <h2><%= article.title %></h2> #Set the title
      <p><%= article.text %></p> #Set the text
    </li>
  <% end %>
</ul>
```

   In this example, we're using the <% @articles.each do |article| %>
   and <% end %> tags to create a loop that iterates over the @articles

119

instance variable (which is set in the controller). For each article, we're using the <%= article.title %> and <%= article.text %> tags to display the title and text of the article.

4. **Start the Server and Visit the Page:** Now, start your Rails server (rails server) and navigate to http://localhost:3000/articles. You should see a list of articles (assuming you have some articles in your database).

Helper Methods for Elegant Views

Rails provides a variety of helper methods that can simplify your view code and make it more readable. Some common helpers include:

- link_to: Creates a link to another page.
- form_with: Creates a form for submitting data.
- image_tag: Displays an image.
- content_tag: Creates an HTML tag with specified content and attributes.

My "View Transformation" Story: I used to write long and convoluted views with a lot of messy Ruby code. But once I discovered view helpers and started using them consistently, my views became much cleaner and more maintainable. It was like I had unlocked a new level of elegance in my code.

Key Takeaways:

- ERB (Embedded Ruby) is a templating language that allows you to embed Ruby code into HTML.
- ERB tags are used to output data, control flow, and add comments.
- You can use instance variables set in the controller to access data in your views.
- Helper methods simplify view code and make it more readable.

By mastering ERB and learning how to use view helpers effectively, you'll be able to create dynamic and visually appealing user interfaces for your Rails applications.

7.2 Layouts and Partials: Build Once, Use Everywhere

You've mastered the basics of creating views with ERB. Now, let's take your view skills to the next level by learning how to create reusable UI components using **layouts** and **partials**.

Think of layouts and partials as your building blocks for constructing complex and consistent user interfaces. They allow you to avoid code duplication, maintain a consistent look and feel across your application, and make your views more modular and manageable.

Layouts: Your Application's Skeleton

A layout is a template that defines the overall structure of your application's pages. Layouts typically include the header, footer, navigation menu, and other common elements that appear on every page. Rails applications use the app/views/layouts/application.html.erb layout by default.

Modifying the Default Layout

Let's start by modifying the default layout to add a header and footer. Open the app/views/layouts/application.html.erb file and add the following code:

```
    <!DOCTYPE html>
<html>
<head>
  <title>My Awesome App</title>
  <%= csrf_meta_tags %>
  <%= stylesheet_link_tag "application", "data-turbo-track":
"reload" %>
  <%= javascript_include_tag "application", "data-turbo-
track": "reload", defer: true %>
</head>

<body>
  <header>
    <h1>My Awesome App</h1>
    <nav>
      <a href="/">Home</a> | <a href="/articles">Articles</a>
    </nav>
  </header>

  <main>
    <%= yield %>
  </main>
```

```
<footer>
  <p>© 2023 My Awesome App</p>
</footer>
</body>
</html>
```

Key points:

- <!DOCTYPE html>, <html>, <head>, <body>: These are standard HTML tags that define the structure of the HTML document.
- <title>My Awesome App</title>: This sets the title of the page.
- <%= csrf_meta_tags %>: This is a Rails helper that includes CSRF (Cross-Site Request Forgery) protection.
- <%= stylesheet_link_tag "application", "data-turbo-track": "reload" %>: This is a Rails helper that includes the application's stylesheet.
- <%= javascript_include_tag "application", "data-turbo-track": "reload", defer: true %>: This is a Rails helper that includes the application's JavaScript files.
- <header>, <nav>, <main>, <footer>: These are semantic HTML5 elements that define the different sections of the page.
- <%= yield %>: This is the most important part of the layout. It tells Rails where to insert the content of the view. Each action has a corresponding view that is rendered here.

Using a Different Layout

To use a different layout for a specific controller action, you can specify the layout option in the controller:

```
class ArticlesController < ApplicationController
layout "special" # use special for every action

def index #If we only want this for the index action, then
add `only: :index`
  @articles = Article.all
end
end
```

This will use the app/views/layouts/special.html.erb layout for all actions in the ArticlesController. This can be helpful if you want to have different layouts for different parts of your application (e.g., a different layout for the admin section).

Partials: Reusable View Snippets

A partial is a smaller template that can be reused in multiple views. Partials are typically used for displaying lists of data, forms, and other common UI elements.

To create a partial, create a new file in the app/views/ directory with a filename that starts with an underscore (_).

Example: Let's create a partial called _article.html.erb that displays the title and content of an article:

```
<h2><%= article.title %></h2>
<p><%= article.text %></p>
```

To render this partial in another view, you can use the render method:

```
<%= render "article", article: @article %> #renders _article.html.erb
```

Key points:

- render "article": This tells Rails to render the _article.html.erb partial.
- article: @article: This passes the @article instance variable to the partial.

Passing Local Variables to Partials

You can also pass local variables to partials using the locals option:

```
<%= render partial: "article", locals: { article: @article, show_comments: true } %> #Pass parameters to the local
```

In the partial, you can then access the local variables using their names:

```
<h2><%= article.title %></h2>
<p><%= article.text %></p>

<% if show_comments %>
  <p>Show comments</p>
<% end %>
```

Collections for DRY (Don't Repeat Yourself)

Partials are great for displaying individual items, but they really shine when rendering collections. Rails provides a shorthand for rendering a collection of items using a partial:

```
<%= render @articles %>
```

This will render the _article.html.erb partial for each article in the @articles collection. Rails automatically infers the partial name and the local variable name based on the collection.

When using this method, you should have a partial called _article and it should use a local variable named article.

My "Partial Victory" Story: I remember struggling with code duplication in my views when I first started learning Rails. I was constantly copying and pasting the same code snippets into different views. Then, I discovered partials, and it was like a lightbulb went off in my head. I could finally create reusable UI components and keep my views clean and organized.

Key Takeaways:

- Layouts define the overall structure of your application's pages.
- Partials are reusable view snippets that can be used in multiple views.
- The render method is used to render partials.
- You can pass local variables to partials using the locals option.

By mastering layouts and partials, you'll be able to create more maintainable, scalable, and visually appealing Rails applications.

7.3 Displaying Model Data: Making Your Data Dance in the Spotlight

You've created your models, connected them to a database, and sculpted the data with migrations. Now, it's time to unveil that data to the world through the magic of Rails views! The view is the place you will show and manipulate the data to output a good looking interface for the end user to view.

Think of this as staging a performance. Your models are the talented actors, and the view is the stage where they strut their stuff, presenting their information in a captivating way.

Setting the Stage: Instance Variables from Controllers

The primary way to pass data from your controllers to your views is through instance variables. Instance variables are variables that start with an @ symbol (e.g., @articles, @user, @product). These variables are accessible within the view that is rendered by the controller action.

Example: Let's say you have an ArticlesController with an index action that retrieves all articles from the database:

```
class ArticlesController < ApplicationController
  def index
    @articles = Article.all #Gets a list of all articles from the database
  end
end
```

In this example, the @articles instance variable is set to the result of Article.all, which retrieves all articles from the database. This instance variable will be available in the app/views/articles/index.html.erb view.

Unveiling the Data in Your Views: ERB to the Rescue

Once you have your instance variables set up in the controller, you can use ERB tags in your views to display the data:

- **Output Tag (<%= ... %>):** This tag evaluates the Ruby code and inserts the result into the HTML output.

Example: Let's display the title and text of each article in the app/views/articles/index.html.erb view:

```
<h1>Listing Articles</h1>

<ul>
```

```
<% @articles.each do |article| %> #Loop each of the
@articles
    <li>
        <h2><%= article.title %></h2> #Shows the article.title
        <p><%= article.text %></p> #shows the text
    </li>
  <% end %>
</ul>
```

In this example:

- <h1>Listing Articles</h1>: This is a standard HTML heading.
- <% @articles.each do |article| %>: This is a Ruby loop that iterates over each article in the @articles instance variable.
- <%= article.title %>: This displays the title of the current article.
- <%= article.text %>: This displays the text of the current article.

Common Data Display Techniques

Here are some common techniques for displaying data in your views:

- **Displaying Simple Attributes:** Use the <%= ... %> tag to directly display the value of an attribute:

```
    <p>Name: <%= @user.name %></p>
<p>Email: <%= @user.email %></p>
```

- **Formatting Data:** Use Ruby methods or Rails helpers to format data before displaying it:

```
    <p>Published on: <%=
@article.created_at.strftime("%m/%d/%Y") %></p> #formats the
article
<p>Price: <%= number_to_currency(@product.price) %></p>
#Formats the price to currency
```

- **Conditional Display:** Use the <% if ... %> tag to conditionally display data:

```
    <% if @user.is_admin? %>
  <p>You have administrator privileges.</p>
<% end %>
```

- **Iterating Over Collections:** Use the <% @collection.each do |item| %> tag to iterate over a collection of items and display data for each item:

```
  <ul>
<% @articles.each do |article| %>
  <li><%= article.title %></li>
<% end %>
</ul>
```

Using View Helpers for a Polished Look

Rails provides a variety of view helpers to simplify common view tasks, such as generating links, creating forms, and formatting data. Using view helpers can make your view code more readable, maintainable, and secure.

Example: Instead of manually creating a link to an article, you can use the link_to helper:

```
<%= link_to "View Article", article_path(@article) %>
```

This will generate an HTML link to the URL for the specified article, using the text "View Article" as the link label.

Security Considerations: Escaping HTML

When displaying data in your views, it's important to be aware of security risks such as cross-site scripting (XSS). XSS attacks occur when malicious code is injected into your web pages, allowing attackers to steal user data or perform other malicious actions.

To prevent XSS attacks, you should always escape HTML entities in user-provided data before displaying it in your views. Rails automatically escapes HTML entities by default, but you can disable this behavior if needed.

My Data Display Transformation Story: I used to just dump raw data into my views without any formatting or styling. The results were often ugly and difficult to read. But as I learned more about view helpers and data formatting techniques, I realized how much of an impact presentation makes. And it's very important to do it!

Key Takeaways:

- Instance variables set in the controller are used to display data in the views.
- ERB tags are used to embed Ruby code into HTML.
- You can use Ruby methods and Rails helpers to format data before displaying it.
- It's important to be aware of security risks such as XSS and to escape HTML entities in user-provided data.

By mastering the art of displaying model data in views, you'll be able to create dynamic, engaging, and secure user interfaces for your Rails applications.

7.4 Helpers: Your Secret Weapon for Clean and Powerful Views

You've learned how to display model data in your views, but as your applications grow in complexity, you'll find yourself writing repetitive code to format data, generate links, and perform other common tasks. This is where *helpers* come to the rescue.

Think of helpers as your toolbox of reusable functions specifically designed to simplify and declutter your views. They allow you to abstract away complex logic, making your views more readable, maintainable, and testable. Also it will help remove a lot of boilerplate code that you would write over and over.

What are Helpers?

Helpers are Ruby modules that define methods that can be used in your views. Rails provides several built-in helpers, and you can also create your own custom helpers to encapsulate application-specific logic.

Built-In Rails Helpers: Your Head Start

Rails comes with a wealth of built-in helpers that cover a wide range of common tasks. Here are some of the most frequently used ones:

- **link_to:** Generates a link to another page.

```
<%= link_to "View Article", article_path(@article) %>
```

- **form_with:** Creates a form for submitting data.

```
<%= form_with(model: @article) do |form| %>
  # Form fields here
<% end %>
```

- **image_tag:** Displays an image.

```
<%= image_tag "logo.png", alt: "My Awesome App" %>
```

- **number_to_currency:** Formats a number as currency.

```
<p>Price: <%= number_to_currency(@product.price) %></p>
```

- **time_ago_in_words:** Displays a time interval in human-readable format.

```
<p>Published <%= time_ago_in_words(@article.created_at) %> ago</p>
```

Creating Your Own Custom Helpers

You can create your own custom helpers to encapsulate application-specific logic. Custom helpers are defined in modules located in the app/helpers/ directory.

Example: Let's create a helper that formats a date in a specific way.

1. **Create a Helper Module:** Create a new file called app/helpers/application_helper.rb (if it doesn't already exist) and add the following code:

```
module ApplicationHelper #Default helper that is automatically created
  def formatted_date(date)
    date.strftime("%m/%d/%Y") #returns string that has the formatted date
  end
```

```
end
```

2. **Use the Helper in Your View:** You can now use the formatted_date helper method in your views:

```
<p>Published on: <%=
formatted_date(@article.created_at) %></p>
```

This will display the creation date of the article in the format MM/DD/YYYY.

Naming Conventions for Helpers

It's a good practice to follow consistent naming conventions for your helper methods. Here are some guidelines:

- Use descriptive names that clearly indicate the purpose of the helper.
- Use snake_case for multi-word helper names (e.g., formatted_date, truncate_text).
- Avoid using generic names that could conflict with other methods.
- Place related helpers in the same module.

Helper Best Practices

- **Keep Helpers Simple:** Helpers should focus on presentation logic. Avoid placing complex business logic in your helpers.
- **Test Your Helpers:** Just like models and controllers, you should test your helpers to ensure that they are working correctly.
- **Use Helpers Consistently:** Once you've created a helper, use it consistently throughout your application to maintain a uniform look and feel.
- **Document Your Helpers:** Add comments to your helper methods to explain their purpose and usage.

Where To Place Helpers?

- **app/helpers/application_helper.rb:** The most common and recommended place for helper functions. Everything defined here will be available throughout all the views.

- **app/helpers/your_controller_name_helper.rb**: If it only relates to a single controller, then creating a specific helper is an appropriate action.

My "Helper Hero" Story: I used to dread writing complex view logic. I always felt like I was repeating myself and making my views more difficult to read. But once I started using helpers consistently, it transformed the way I approached view development. My views became cleaner, more organized, and easier to maintain, and I could focus on the presentation of the data rather than the low-level details.

Key Takeaways:

- Helpers are Ruby modules that define methods that can be used in your views.
- Rails provides several built-in helpers that cover a wide range of common tasks.
- You can create your own custom helpers to encapsulate application-specific logic.
- Keep helpers simple, test them, use them consistently, and document them.

By mastering helpers, you'll be able to create more elegant, maintainable, and testable views for your Rails applications. It's a skill that will significantly boost your productivity and make view development a more enjoyable experience.

7.5 Asset Pipeline Basics: Styling and Scripting Your Rails Applications

You've built models, views, and controllers, and you're creating dynamic web pages. Now, it's time to add the finishing touches: styling with CSS and interactivity with JavaScript. The Rails *Asset Pipeline* is the framework that manages these assets, making it easier to organize, optimize, and deliver them to your users.

Think of the Asset Pipeline as your personal stylist and stage manager. It ensures that your application looks its best and that all the elements are in place for a smooth and engaging user experience.

What is the Asset Pipeline?

The Asset Pipeline is a set of tools and conventions that Rails uses to manage assets such as CSS, JavaScript, and images. It provides features such as:

- **Concatenation:** Combines multiple asset files into a single file to reduce the number of HTTP requests.
- **Minification:** Removes unnecessary characters from asset files to reduce their size.
- **Compression:** Compresses asset files to further reduce their size.
- **Fingerprinting:** Adds a unique hash to the filename of each asset to enable browser caching and prevent stale assets from being used.

Why Use the Asset Pipeline?

- **Improved Performance:** The Asset Pipeline reduces the number of HTTP requests, reduces the size of asset files, and enables browser caching, all of which improve the performance of your application.
- **Code Organization:** The Asset Pipeline provides a clear and consistent way to organize your asset files.
- **Automation:** The Asset Pipeline automates many of the tasks involved in managing assets, such as concatenation, minification, and fingerprinting.

The Core Directories

The Asset Pipeline uses three primary directories for storing asset files:

- app/assets/: This is where you store the assets that are specific to your application. This includes CSS files, JavaScript files, image files, and font files.
- lib/assets/: This is where you store assets that are shared between multiple applications. This is typically used for libraries and plugins that you want to reuse across multiple projects.
- vendor/assets/: This is where you store assets that are provided by third-party vendors, such as CSS frameworks and JavaScript libraries. This is typically where you would copy the files if you were not using a CSS or Javascript bundler.

Referencing Assets in Your Views

In your views, you can use the following helper methods to reference asset files:

- stylesheet_link_tag: Generates a link to a CSS file.

  ```
  <%= stylesheet_link_tag "application" %>
  ```

- javascript_include_tag: Generates a script tag to include a JavaScript file.

  ```
  <%= javascript_include_tag "application" %>
  ```

- image_tag: Generates an image tag to display an image.

  ```
  <%= image_tag "logo.png", alt: "My Awesome App" %>
  ```

These helper methods automatically generate the correct paths to your asset files, taking into account the asset pipeline's transformations (concatenation, minification, fingerprinting).

CSS and JavaScript Bundlers

Rails uses a set of command to compile assets. By default if you just add the file to the asset folder, rails will concat them, but it may be harder to load the different libraries that are being used. To assist, the bundlers can be used.

A Javascript and CSS bundler helps with loading a javascript or CSS framework and their dependency. It helps organize a more complex front end application. The most commonly used bundlers in Rails are webpacker (currently deprecated, but still very frequently used), and jsbundling-rails with esbuild or importmap.

Webpacker is deprecated for Rails 7.1 and will not be supported past Rails 8

- jsbundling-rails
  This is the "Rails way" to add javascript.
  It supports three strategies:

133

1. esbuild - Build javascript using esbuild.
2. rollup - Build javascript using rollup.
3. importmap - Use the browser's native importmap support.

- cssbundling-rails
  Similar to above, is the "Rails way" to add CSS.
  It supports three strategies:

1. tailwind - Use the Tailwind CSS framework.
2. bootstrap - Use the Bootstrap CSS framework.
3. sass - Use the Sass CSS preprocessor

If using one of the bundler systems, then you do not add your javascript or CSS directly to the view, but will load the bundler file on the view.

The Asset Pipeline in Production

In the production environment, the Asset Pipeline performs several additional steps to optimize your assets for deployment:

- **Precompilation:** The Asset Pipeline precompiles all of your assets into a set of static files. These static files are then served directly by the web server, without having to go through the Rails application.
- **Fingerprinting:** The Asset Pipeline adds a unique hash to the filename of each asset. This allows the browser to cache the asset file indefinitely, as the filename will change whenever the content of the asset file changes.

To precompile your assets in production, run the following command:

```
rails assets:precompile
```

This will create a directory called public/assets that contains all of your precompiled assets.

My Asset Pipeline Enlightenment Story: I used to dread dealing with assets in web development. It always seemed like a confusing mess of files and dependencies. But once I learned about the Rails Asset Pipeline, it transformed the way I approached asset management. The Asset Pipeline made it easy to organize, optimize, and deploy my assets, and it significantly improved the performance of my applications.

Key Takeaways:

- The Asset Pipeline manages assets such as CSS, JavaScript, and images.
- The Asset Pipeline provides features such as concatenation, minification, compression, and fingerprinting.
- Use stylesheet_link_tag, javascript_include_tag, and image_tag to reference asset files in your views.
- Use webpacker, jsbundling-rails, and cssbundling-rails to better manage your asset and code files

By understanding the basics of the Rails Asset Pipeline, you'll be able to optimize your application's performance and create more visually appealing and engaging user interfaces.

Chapter 8: Controllers and Routing: The Traffic Cops of Your Web App

You've learned how to build models, create views, and manage your assets. Now, it's time to connect everything together and learn how to handle user requests. This is where *controllers* and *routing* come into play.

Think of controllers and routing as the traffic cops of your web application. They direct the flow of traffic, ensuring that each request reaches its destination and that the appropriate response is sent back to the user.

8.1 Controllers: Your Application's Central Command

You've connected your models and created views to showcase the data. Now comes the glue that links them together: the controller. In Rails, controllers are the central processing units of your application, responsible for handling user requests, interacting with models to fetch or manipulate data, and then deciding which view to render to present the results. They truly control the flow.

Think of a controller as the director of a play. The director receives the script (the user request), works with the actors (the models) to rehearse the scenes, and then presents the final performance (the view) to the audience.

What are Controllers?

Controllers are Ruby classes that inherit from ApplicationController (located in app/controllers/application_controller.rb). They reside in the app/controllers/ directory. Each controller typically manages a specific resource or a set of related resources in your application (e.g., ArticlesController for articles, UsersController for users).

Actions: Handling Specific Requests

A controller is composed of several methods, known as *actions*. Each action is responsible for handling a specific type of request (e.g., displaying a list of articles, creating a new article, updating an existing article). The name of the action corresponds to the URL that is used to access it.

Generating a Controller

Rails provides a generator to quickly create controllers and their associated files:

```
rails generate controller Articles index show new
create edit update destroy
```

This command will generate:

- app/controllers/articles_controller.rb: The controller file.
- app/views/articles/index.html.erb, app/views/articles/show.html.erb, etc.: View files for each action.
- app/helpers/articles_helper.rb: A helper file (we'll discuss this later).
- test/controllers/articles_controller_test.rb: A test file (we'll discuss testing in a later chapter).
- Modifications to config/routes.rb: This automatically maps the correct URLs to point to this new controller.

You can also generate a controller with only specific actions:

```
rails generate controller Articles index show
```

This will only generate the index and show actions and their corresponding view files.

Anatomy of a Controller Action

Let's examine a typical controller action:

```
class ArticlesController < ApplicationController #Model
inhereting from the Application Controller
  def index #A method in the model
    @articles = Article.all #Sets the instance variable to
the list of all articles
  end

  def show
    @article = Article.find(params[:id]) #Find a single
article by id, sets the instance variable
  end
end
```

Let's break down the key components:

- class ArticlesController < ApplicationController: This defines a controller called ArticlesController that inherits from ApplicationController.
- def index: This defines an action called index.
- @articles = Article.all: This retrieves all articles from the database using the Article model and assigns them to the @articles instance variable. This instance variable will be available in the view.
- def show: An action that uses Article.find(params[:id]) to get a single record from the database. This uses the params method to grab the article by ID

Important Concepts

- **Instance Variables (@variables):** These are the primary way to pass data from the controller to the view. They are accessible within the view template.
- **params Hash:** This hash contains all the parameters that are passed to the controller, either in the URL (query parameters) or in the request body (form data). The params[:id] gives the ID in a GET or DELETE action.
- **render Method:** This method tells Rails which view to render. If you don't explicitly call render, Rails will automatically render a view with the same name as the action (e.g., app/views/articles/index.html.erb for the index action).

Using before_action Filters

You can use before_action filters to execute code before specific actions in your controller. This is often used to perform tasks such as authentication, authorization, or data preparation.

Example: Let's say you want to ensure that a user is logged in before they can access any of the actions in the ArticlesController. You can add a before_action filter to the controller:

```
class ArticlesController < ApplicationController
  before_action :authenticate_user! #Requires the user to authenticate to access. This is Devise syntax.
  before_action :set_article, only: [:show, :edit, :update, :destroy] #Runs set_article method before show, edit, update, and destroy
```

```
  private

  def set_article
    @article = Article.find(params[:id])
  end
end
```

Then you can only access those methods after using devise.

Controller Best Practices

- **Keep Controllers Lean:** Controllers should focus on handling requests, interacting with models, and selecting views. Avoid placing complex business logic in your controllers.
- **Use Instance Variables Wisely:** Use instance variables to pass data to the view, but avoid creating too many instance variables.
- **Follow RESTful Conventions:** Use RESTful routing and HTTP verbs to create well-organized and predictable URLs.
- **Test Your Controllers:** Write tests for your controllers to ensure that they are handling requests correctly and interacting with the models appropriately.

My "Controller Conundrum" Story: I used to cram all sorts of logic into my controllers, making them bloated and difficult to maintain. Then I learned about the importance of keeping controllers lean and delegating business logic to the models. It transformed the way I approached controller development and made my code much more organized and manageable.

Key Takeaways:

- Controllers handle user requests and coordinate between models and views.
- Actions are methods within a controller that handle specific requests.
- The params hash contains the parameters that are passed to the controller.
- The render method tells Rails which view to render.
- before_action filters can be used to execute code before specific actions.

By mastering controllers and actions, you'll be able to build dynamic and interactive web applications that respond to user input and provide a seamless user experience. This is a fundamental skill for any Rails developer!

8.2 Defining Routes: Your Application's Street Address System

You've created controllers and actions to handle user requests. Now, you need to define the *routes* that map URLs to those controller actions. Think of routes as the street address system for your application. When a user visits a specific URL, the router acts like the postal service, figuring out which controller and action should handle the request.

Proper routing is crucial for creating a well-organized, predictable, and user-friendly web application. It's what allows users to navigate your site, access specific resources, and interact with your application's features.

The config/routes.rb File: Your Routing Table

The routes for your Rails application are defined in the config/routes.rb file. This file contains a set of rules that specify how URLs are mapped to controller actions.

The Basic Syntax: HTTP Verbs and URLs

The basic syntax for defining a route in config/routes.rb is:

```
HTTP_VERB 'URL', to: 'controller#action'
```

- HTTP_VERB: This specifies the HTTP verb that the route should match. The most common HTTP verbs are get, post, put, patch, and delete.
- 'URL': This specifies the URL pattern that the route should match. The URL pattern can contain placeholders for dynamic segments (e.g., /:id).
- to: 'controller#action': This specifies the controller and action that should handle the request when the route matches.

Common HTTP Verbs and Their Meanings

- **get:** Used to retrieve a resource (e.g., display a list of articles, display a specific article).
- **post:** Used to create a new resource (e.g., create a new article, submit a form).
- **put:** Used to completely update an existing resource.
- **patch:** Used to partially update an existing resource.
- delete: Used to delete a resource.

RESTful Routing: A Standardized Approach

Rails promotes the use of RESTful routing, which is a set of conventions for mapping HTTP verbs to controller actions in a consistent and predictable way. RESTful routing makes it easier to create well-organized and maintainable web APIs.

The resources Method: Your RESTful Shortcut

Rails provides the resources method as a convenient way to generate a set of RESTful routes for a controller. Instead of writing each action one by one.

```
      resources :articles #Tells Rails to create routes for
the articles resource
```

This single line generates the following routes:

- GET /articles: articles#index (Displays a list of all articles)
- GET /articles/new: articles#new (Displays a form for creating a new article)
- POST /articles: articles#create (Creates a new article)
- GET /articles/:id: articles#show (Displays a specific article)
- GET /articles/:id/edit: articles#edit (Displays a form for editing an existing article)
- PUT /articles/:id: articles#update (Updates an existing article)
- DELETE /articles/:id: articles#destroy (Deletes an article)

When clicking and doing an action, you have to be sure it's the right verb, so it follows this table. The views should post (create), get, put, or delete the correct action so that the router knows what to do.

Beyond Resources: Custom Routes for Unique Cases

While resources covers a lot of ground, you'll inevitably encounter situations where you need custom routes that don't fit the RESTful mold. In these cases, you can define routes individually using get, post, put, patch, and delete.

Example: A custom search route

```
get '/articles/search', to: 'articles#search', as: 'article_search'
```

Important aspects of this line:

- get '/articles/search': This specifies a GET route for the URL /articles/search.
- to: 'articles#search': This tells Rails to dispatch requests to this URL to the search action of the ArticlesController.
- as: 'article_search': This creates a named route helper called article_search_path (and article_search_url), which you can use in your views and controllers to generate the URL for this route. This is optional.

Using Route Helpers: Keeping Your Code DRY (Don't Repeat Yourself)

Rails automatically generates route helpers for each route that you define. Route helpers are methods that generate the URL for a specific route.

Using route helpers makes your code more readable, maintainable, and less prone to errors. If you change the URL for a route, you only need to update the route definition in config/routes.rb, and all the corresponding route helpers will be updated automatically.

To see a list of all the route helpers that are available in your application, you can run the rails routes command:

```
rails routes
```

This will display a table of all the routes in your application, including the HTTP verb, URL pattern, controller action, and route helper name.

Setting the Root Route: Welcoming Your Users

142

You can set the root route for your application, which is the URL that users will see when they visit your application's domain name.

```
root 'welcome#index'
```

This will map the root URL (/) to the index action of the WelcomeController.

My "Routing Revelation" Story: I used to create a bunch of custom routes without really understanding the power of RESTful conventions. One day, I realized that RESTful routing made my URLs more predictable, easier to understand, and better aligned with web standards. It was a moment where I started thinking about code design and the way things should work.

Key Takeaways:

- Routes map URLs to controller actions.
- The config/routes.rb file defines the routes for your application.
- The resources method generates a set of RESTful routes for a controller.
- You can define custom routes using get, post, put, patch, and delete.
- Route helpers make your code more readable, maintainable, and less prone to errors.

By mastering routes, you'll be able to create a well-organized and user-friendly web application that is easy to navigate and understand. It's the foundation that makes your web pages accessible and easy to use.

8.3 Passing Data Between Controllers and Views: The Message Delivery System

You've learned how to create controllers, define actions, and set up routes. Now, let's explore one of the most fundamental aspects of web development: how to pass data from your controllers to your views. This data is how you display the information to the end users on the screen.

Think of this process as delivering a message. The controller is the sender of the message, and the view is the recipient. The controller needs to package the data (the message) and send it to the view in a way that it can be easily accessed and displayed.

Instance Variables: Your Data Messengers

The primary way to pass data from controllers to views in Rails is through *instance variables*. Instance variables are variables that start with an @ symbol (e.g., @articles, @user, @product). Instance variables are accessible within the view that is rendered by the controller action.

Using Instance Variables to send data ensures that the information reaches the views where users interact with the application and can do more tasks. It also helps separate the actions and tasks performed by a controller and the visuals that the user will see.

Setting Instance Variables in the Controller

Inside your controller actions, you assign values to instance variables. These values can be any Ruby object, such as strings, numbers, arrays, hashes, or even other models.

Example: Let's say you have an ArticlesController with an index action that retrieves all articles from the database:

```ruby
class ArticlesController < ApplicationController
  def index
    @articles = Article.all
  end
end
```

In this example, the @articles instance variable is set to the result of Article.all, which retrieves all articles from the database.

Accessing Data in Your Views

In your views, you can access the values of instance variables using ERB tags. For example, in the app/views/articles/index.html.erb view, you can iterate over the @articles instance variable and display the title of each article:

```erb
<h1>Listing Articles</h1>

<ul>
  <% @articles.each do |article| %>
    <li><%= article.title %></li>
  <% end %>
```

```
</ul>
```

Using <%=...%> syntax can be used to display any property or method inside the controller.

A More Complex Example: Displaying Article Details

Let's create a more complex example that displays the title, text, and author of a specific article.

1. **Model (Article):** We need to create a model so that we have data to pass.

```
class Article < ApplicationRecord #This is a model
  validates :title, presence: true, length: { minimum: 5 }
#Requires the title to be present, and have a minimum of 5
characters
  validates :text, presence: true #requires the text to be
present
end
```

1. **Controller:** We also need to set it up in our route and create a controller.

```
class ArticlesController < ApplicationController

  def show #Action is invoked by the route to the action
    @article = Article.find(params[:id]) #Find a single
article by id, sets the instance variable
  end
end
```

1. Then we need to set up a route, such as resources :articles
2. **View (app/views/articles/show.html.erb):**

```
<h1><%= @article.title %></h1> #Displays the title of
the page
<p><%= @article.text %></p>  #Displays the test of the page.
```

In this example:

- We set the @article instance variable to the result of Article.find(params[:id]), which retrieves a specific article from the database based on its ID.
- In the view, we use the <%= @article.title %> and <%= @article.text %> tags to display the title and text of the article.

Other Ways to Pass Data (Less Common)

While instance variables are the primary way to pass data from controllers to views, there are a few other ways to pass data:

- **content_for:** If you need to define content that is displayed in a specific region of the layout, you can use content_for.
- **Helpers:** Helpers are modules that define methods that can be used in your views. You can pass data to helpers as arguments to the helper methods.

However, these methods are less commonly used and are typically reserved for more advanced scenarios. Instance variables are the most straightforward and widely used approach.

Security Considerations: Sanitizing User Input

When displaying data in your views, it's essential to be aware of security risks, such as cross-site scripting (XSS). Always sanitize user input with the sanitize helper before rendering it.

Best Practices

- Use instance variables to pass data from controllers to views.
- Keep your controllers lean and focused on handling requests and preparing data.
- Use view helpers to format and display data in your views.
- Be aware of security risks such as XSS and sanitize user input before displaying it.

My "Data Delivery" Success Story: I used to struggle with passing data between controllers and views. I would often end up with messy and hard-to-read code that was difficult to maintain. But once I understood the power and simplicity of instance variables, it transformed the way I approached view development. My code became more organized, more readable, and easier to test.

Key Takeaways:

- Instance variables are the primary way to pass data from controllers to views.
- Set instance variables in your controller actions to make them available in your views.
- Access instance variables in your views using ERB tags.

By mastering the art of passing data between controllers and views, you'll be able to create dynamic, interactive, and user-friendly web applications that bring your data to life.

8.4 Working with Parameters (Params): Capturing User Intent

You've learned how to route requests to controllers and pass data to views. Now, let's explore how to capture data that users send *to* your application through parameters. Parameters (often shortened to "params") are key-value pairs that are passed from the client (e.g., a web browser) to the server as part of an HTTP request. This is how users interact with forms, pass data to search queries, and generally tell your application what they want to do.

Think of parameters as the user's instructions to your application. They provide the context and information that your application needs to fulfill the user's request.

Where do Parameters Come From?

Parameters can come from several sources:

- **Query Parameters:** These are appended to the URL after a question mark (?). They are used for passing data with GET requests (e.g., http://example.com/articles?search=keyword&page=2).
- **Form Data:** When a user submits a form, the data is typically sent in the body of the request, using either POST or PUT/PATCH methods. The form data is encoded in a specific format (e.g., application/x-www-form-urlencoded or multipart/form-data).
- **URL Segments:** You can define routes with dynamic segments in the URL, which are captured as parameters. For example, a route like /articles/:id will capture the value of the :id segment as a parameter.

Accessing Parameters in Your Controller

In your Rails controllers, you can access all the parameters that were sent with the request using the params hash. The params hash is a special object that provides access to all the parameters, regardless of their source.

Example: Let's say you have a search form that submits a query parameter to the /articles/search URL. In the search action of your ArticlesController, you can access the query parameter like this:

```
    class ArticlesController < ApplicationController
  def search
    @query = params[:query] #Gets the query parameter
    @articles = Article.where("title LIKE ?", "%#{@query}%")
#Performs a search with the extracted query.
    render :index
  end
end
```

Here @query refers to the search string that was inputted by the user. The value will be set to whatever the user typed in.

Security Note: Never trust user input directly. Always sanitize and validate user input before using it in your application, especially when interacting with the database.

Using Strong Parameters

Rails provides a feature called *strong parameters* to help protect your application from mass assignment vulnerabilities. Mass assignment occurs when a malicious user can manipulate the parameters that are submitted with a form, potentially setting attributes on your model that they shouldn't be able to access.

Strong parameters allow you to specify which attributes are permitted to be set on your model. Any attributes that are not explicitly permitted will be ignored.

Example: Let's say you have an Article model with title, text, and published attributes. You only want users to be able to set the title and text attributes. You can use strong parameters to achieve this:

```
    class ArticlesController < ApplicationController

  def create
```

```
  @article = Article.new(article_params)

  if @article.save
    redirect_to @article
  else
    render :new
  end
end

private
  def article_params #Sets the properties that can be set
for the user,
    params.require(:article).permit(:title, :text)
#Requires article as a main parameter, and text or title can
be passed. All other parameters will throw an error.
  end
end
```

Here's a breakdown:

- params.require(:article): This ensures that the params hash contains a key called article. If the article key is missing, it will raise an exception.
- permit(:title, :text): This specifies that only the title and text attributes are permitted. Any other attributes that are submitted in the params hash will be ignored.

Form Helpers and Parameter Names

Rails provides form helpers that automatically generate the correct parameter names for your form fields. When using form helpers, the parameter names will typically follow this convention:

```
<input type="text" name="article[title]">
<textarea name="article[text]"></textarea>
```

In this example, the parameter names are article[title] and article[text]. This means that the params hash will contain a key called article, which will be a hash containing the title and text attributes.

My "Parameter Pitfall" Story: I once forgot to use strong parameters in a Rails application and accidentally exposed a sensitive attribute to mass assignment. A malicious user was able to manipulate the parameters and set that attribute, causing a security breach. I learned the hard way that strong parameters are essential for protecting your application from security vulnerabilities.

Key Takeaways:

- Parameters are key-value pairs that are passed from the client to the server.
- The params hash provides access to all the parameters that were sent with the request.
- Strong parameters allow you to specify which attributes are permitted to be set on your model.
- Always sanitize and validate user input before using it in your application.

By mastering parameters and strong parameters, you'll be able to build secure and robust Rails applications that can effectively capture and process user input.

8.5 RESTful Routing: Building Web APIs the Right Way

You've learned the basics of routing in Rails. Now, let's explore a powerful and widely adopted architectural style for designing web APIs: **REST (Representational State Transfer)**. RESTful routing is a set of conventions that guides you in mapping HTTP verbs (GET, POST, PUT, PATCH, DELETE) to controller actions in a consistent and predictable way.

Think of RESTful routing as a blueprint for organizing your web application's URLs and actions. It provides a clear and standardized approach that makes your application easier to understand, maintain, and integrate with other systems.

What is REST?

REST is an architectural style for building distributed systems, such as web APIs. It emphasizes the use of standard HTTP verbs to perform operations on resources.

Key principles of REST:

- **Resources:** Everything in a RESTful API is treated as a resource. A resource can be anything that can be identified by a URL, such as a user, an article, a product, or an image.
- **Representations:** Resources can have multiple representations, such as HTML, JSON, XML, or plain text. The client can specify the desired representation using the Accept header.
- **Statelessness:** The server does not store any state about the client between requests. Each request from the client must contain all the information that the server needs to fulfill the request.
- **Uniform Interface:** The API should have a consistent and predictable interface. Clients should be able to understand how to interact with the API without having to read extensive documentation.
- **HTTP Verbs:** HTTP verbs (GET, POST, PUT, PATCH, DELETE) are used to perform operations on resources.

RESTful Routing in Rails: Mapping Verbs to Actions

Rails provides a set of conventions for mapping HTTP verbs to controller actions in a RESTful way. The resources method in config/routes.rb is the primary tool for generating RESTful routes:

```
resources :articles
```

This single line generates the following routes:

HTTP Verb	URL	Controller Action	Description
GET	/articles	articles#index	Displays a list of all articles
GET	/articles/new	articles#new	Displays a form for creating a new article
POST	/articles	articles#create	Creates a new article
GET	/articles/:id	articles#show	Displays a specific article
GET	/articles/:id/edit	articles#edit	Displays a form for editing an existing article
PUT	/articles/:id	articles#update	Updates an existing article completely
PATCH	/articles/:id	articles#update	Partially updates an existing article

DELETE   /articles/:id   articles#destroy   Deletes an article

Let's analyze each of these methods:

1. GET - getting a resource. When wanting to request data, it makes sense to use a GET request. The controller action would usually use a method like find to display the data.
2. POST - creating a resource. Often this involves a form where users input the information. Then the controller action takes the data and saves it.
3. PUT/PATCH - both are about updating an existing resource. Typically you would only want to update all aspects of the information using PUT, and use PATCH to update a small amount of aspects.
4. DELETE - is used to delete a resource. This action typically renders nothing.

Why RESTful Routing Matters

- **Predictability:** RESTful URLs are easy to understand and predict.
- **Consistency:** RESTful routing provides a consistent interface for interacting with your application.
- **Discoverability:** RESTful URLs are discoverable. Clients can easily navigate your API by following links and understanding the relationships between resources.
- **Scalability:** RESTful APIs are designed to be scalable and can handle large volumes of traffic.
- **Interoperability:** RESTful APIs are based on standard HTTP protocols, making them easy to integrate with other systems.

Non-RESTful Actions

There are situations where the actions to be performed don't fall into one of the four actions above. Sometimes they are actions that you can call that do not touch the base model. For example, creating an action to search:

```
get 'articles/search', to: 'articles#search', as:
'article_search'
```

By including this, it is easy to add a new way to access resources while still conforming to good design practices.

My "RESTful Conversion" Story: When I first started building web applications, I didn't pay much attention to the design of my URLs. I just created routes as I needed them, without any real structure or consistency. But as I learned more about RESTful routing, I realized how much it improved the organization and maintainability of my applications. It became an essential part of my web development toolkit.

Key Takeaways:

- RESTful routing is a set of conventions for mapping HTTP verbs to controller actions in a consistent and predictable way.
- The resources method is used to generate a set of RESTful routes for a controller.
- HTTP verbs (GET, POST, PUT, PATCH, DELETE) are used to perform operations on resources.

By understanding and applying the principles of RESTful routing, you'll be able to create well-designed and standards-compliant web APIs that are easy to understand, maintain, and integrate with other systems.

Chapter 9: Working with Forms: Gathering User Insights

You've learned how to display data to users, but what about capturing data *from* them? That's where *forms* come in. Forms are the primary way that users interact with your application, providing a way to submit data, search for information, and perform various actions.

Think of forms as a two-way conversation between your application and its users. The application presents the form, and the user responds by filling it out and submitting it.

9.1 Building Forms with Rails Form Helpers: Your Digital Questionnaire

Forms are the lifeblood of any interactive web application. They allow users to provide information, express their preferences, and interact with your application in a meaningful way. And as a developer, you will most likely need a form for most pages that you will display!

Think of forms as digital questionnaires. They ask users for specific information and then collect their responses for processing.

Rails provides a powerful set of form helpers that greatly simplify the process of creating HTML forms. These helpers automatically generate the necessary HTML code, handle data binding, and integrate seamlessly with your models.

Why Use Form Helpers?

- **Code Generation:** Form helpers automatically generate the HTML code for your form fields, saving you time and effort.
- **Data Binding:** Form helpers automatically bind your form fields to the attributes of your model, making it easier to process user input.
- **Security:** Form helpers help you protect your application from security vulnerabilities by automatically escaping user input.
- **Consistency:** Form helpers ensure that your forms have a consistent look and feel throughout your application.

The form_with Helper: The Modern Standard

The form_with helper is the recommended way to create forms in Rails 6 and later. It provides a unified interface for creating forms that submit data to both regular controllers and API controllers. It replaces older helpers like form_for and form_tag. It also handles all of the heavy liftings of generating the HTML scaffolding and connecting the information for you.

Basic Syntax

```
<%= form_with(model: @article) do |form| %>
  # Form fields here
<% end %>
```

Let's break down this code:

- form_with(model: @article): This creates a new form builder, with the code block.
- model: @article: This specifies the model that the form is associated with. In this case, the form is associated with the @article instance variable, which should be an instance of your Article model. If the @article object exists (i.e., you are updating a record), the form will automatically populate the fields with the existing values. If the @article object is new (i.e., you are creating a new record), the form will generate empty fields.
- do |form|: This creates a block that yields a form object. The form object is used to generate the form fields.

Key Benefit: By associating the form with a model using model: @article, Rails automatically sets up the form to submit data to the correct controller action and with the appropriate parameter names.

Generating Form Fields with the form Object

The form object provides a set of methods for generating different types of form fields. The most common field types are:

- **Text Fields:** Used for single-line text input.

```
<%= form.label :title %><br>
<%= form.text_field :title %>
```

- **Text Areas:** Used for multi-line text input.

```
    <%= form.label :text %><br>
<%= form.text_area :text %>
```

- **Select Boxes:** Used to choose a list of options

```
    <%= form.label :title %><br>
    <%= form.select :category, ["news", "sports",
"entertainment"] %>
```

- **Check Boxes:** Used to select a boolean (true/false) option.

```
    <%= form.label :published %><br>
    <%= form.check_box :published %>
```

- **Radio Buttons:** Used to select one option from a group of options.

```
    <%= form.label :title %><br>
<%= form.radio_button :format, "html" %> HTML
<%= form.radio_button :format, "pdf" %> PDF
```

- **File Fields:** Used to upload files.

```
    <%- form.label :image %><br>
  <%= form.file_field :image %>
```

- **Hidden Fields:** Used to store data that is not displayed to the user.

```
    <%= form.hidden_field :user_id, value: @user.id %>
```

- **Dates and Times**
  You can also specify the date and time if it's a single choice, or multiple boxes, that show the date and the time to the end user.

```
    <%= form.date_field :publish_date %>
    <%= form.datetime_field :start_time %>
```

Labels and Hints

It's a good practice to add labels to your form fields to provide context to the user. You can use the label method to generate a label for a form field:

```
    <%= form.label :title, "Article Title" %>
<%= form.text_field :title %>
```

The Submit Button

Every form needs a submit button to allow the user to submit the data. You can use the submit method to generate a submit button:

```
    <%= form.submit "Create Article" %>
```

The submit method takes an optional argument that specifies the text to display on the button.

Example: A Complete Form

Let's put it all together and create a complete form for creating a new Article object:

```
    <h1>New Article</h1>

<%= form_with(model: @article) do |form| %>
  <div>
    <%= form.label :title %><br>
    <%= form.text_field :title %>
  </div>

  <div>
    <%= form.label :text %><br>
    <%= form.text_area :text %>
  </div>
  <div>
      <%= form.label :category %><br>
      <%= form.select :category, ["news", "sports",
"entertainment"] %>
    </div>
  <div>
      <%= form.label :published %><br>
      <%= form.check_box :published %>
  </div>
  <div>
     <%= form.label :image %><br>
     <%= form.file_field :image %>
```

```
    </div>

  <div>
    <%= form.submit "Create Article" %>
  </div>
<% end %>
```

My "Formative" Form Experience: When I first started using Rails, forms seemed like a necessary evil. But once I discovered the power and convenience of form helpers, I realized how much easier and more enjoyable form development could be. I could quickly create complex forms with minimal code and focus on the user experience rather than the low-level details of HTML.

Key Takeaways:

- Rails form helpers simplify the process of creating HTML forms.
- The form_with helper is the recommended way to create forms in Rails 6 and later.
- The form object provides a set of methods for generating different types of form fields.
- Labels and hints provide context to the user.
- The submit method generates a submit button.

By mastering form helpers, you'll be able to create dynamic and user-friendly forms that capture the data you need and provide a great user experience. This is a fundamental skill for any Rails developer!

9.2 Processing Form Submissions: Harvesting User Data

You've learned how to create forms that allow users to enter data. Now, it's time to explore how to process those form submissions and extract the data that users send to your application. This is a critical step in any web application, as it allows you to capture user input, store it in your database, and respond to user actions.

Think of this as harvesting the fruits of your labor. You've planted the seeds (created the form), and now it's time to gather the harvest (process the form submission).

The create Action: Your Form Processing Hub

The controller action that is responsible for processing form submissions is typically the create action. This action is invoked when the user submits a form using the POST method. It receives all the data from the form in the params hash.

Example: Let's say you have an ArticlesController with a create action that processes the submission of a new article:

```
    class ArticlesController < ApplicationController

  def create #action to process the form
    @article = Article.new(article_params)

    if @article.save #if the model saves successfully, return
the link
      redirect_to @article
    else #Other wise render the page
      render :new
    end
  end
end
```

In this example:

- def create: This defines the create action.
- @article = Article.new(article_params): This creates a new Article object using the data from the params hash. You will also need to define a private method that allows access to certain attributes that were entered in the model. Read about Strong Parameters below
- @article.save: This saves the Article object to the database. If the save is successful, the method returns the link. If there are errors, the user is returned back to the view to correct.
- redirect_to @article: This redirects the user to the show action for the newly created article.
- render :new: This renders the new view again, allowing the user to correct any errors.

The update Action: Processing Updates

For update forms, the action you use to process it will typically be the update action.

```
    def update
```

```
  if @article.update(article_params) #If it succesfully saves
the model with the new parameters, then return.
    redirect_to @article
  else
    render :edit, status: :unprocessable_entity #if that did
not work, then show the page again
  end
end
```

Accessing Form Data with the params Hash

As you know, the params hash is how you can access the values and information that were entered on the page. The values are structured as key/value pairs, which are sent on submission of the form.

To access parameters, you would specify a particular field using either a symbol or a string. For example,

```
    @article[:title]
  @article["title"]
```

However, for security reasons, you should only allow certain attributes to be set.

Using Strong Parameters for Security

Mass assignment is one of the biggest vulnerability that comes with these code designs. It allows users to send any field from the view and set it on the model. But we wouldn't want end users to set properties that they should not be able to.

As a result, Rails introduced "Strong Parameters" where only approved properties are allowed to be set with a private model in the controller.

```
    private
  def article_params
    params.require(:article).permit(:title, :text)
  end
```

Let's break down this code:

160

- params.require(:article): This ensures that the params hash contains a key called article. This is a way to protect your application from malicious requests that might try to set other parameters on your model.
- permit(:title, :text): This specifies that only the title and text attributes are permitted. Any other attributes that are submitted in the params hash will be ignored.

Responding to Successful Submissions

After successfully saving the data to the database, you typically want to redirect the user to another page. Rails provides several ways to redirect users:

- redirect_to @article: This redirects the user to the show action for the specified article. Rails automatically generates the correct URL based on the model's ID.
- redirect_to articles_path: This redirects the user to the index action for the ArticlesController.
- redirect_to root_path: This redirects the user to the root URL of your application.

Handling Validation Errors

If there are any validation errors when you try to save the model, the save method will return false. In this case, you typically want to re-render the form, displaying the validation errors to the user.

```
    def create #action to process the form
  @article = Article.new(article_params)

    if @article.save #if the model saves successfully, return
the link
      redirect_to @article
    else #Other wise render the page
      render :new, status: :unprocessable_entity #status
allows you to customize, such as to show 400 in case there
was an error
    end
  end
```

This will re-render the new view, displaying the validation errors to the user. We'll cover how to display validation errors in more detail in the next section.

My "Formidable Data" Story: I remember the first time I successfully processed a form submission in Rails. It felt like I had unlocked a new level of power and control over my application. I could finally capture user input, store it in the database, and respond to user actions in a meaningful way. The key here is the security aspect with being able to know which properties the user can change and protecting other properties.

Key Takeaways:

- The create action is typically responsible for processing form submissions.
- The params hash provides access to all the parameters that were sent with the request.
- Always use strong parameters to protect your application from mass assignment vulnerabilities.
- Redirect the user to another page after successfully saving the data.
- Re-render the form with error messages if there are validation errors.

By mastering form submissions, you'll be able to create dynamic and interactive web applications that can effectively capture and process user input.

9.3 Strong Parameters: Your Application's Security Firewall

You've learned how to create forms and process form submissions. Now, let's talk about security. One of the most important security considerations when working with forms is to protect your application from mass assignment vulnerabilities.

Think of strong parameters as a security firewall that protects your models from unauthorized attribute updates. They allow you to explicitly specify which attributes can be set by the user, preventing malicious users from manipulating your data.

What is Mass Assignment?

Mass assignment is a feature of Active Record (Rails' ORM) that allows you to set multiple attributes on a model at once using a hash of key-value pairs. For example:

```
@user = User.new(params[:user])
```

This code creates a new User object using the data from the params[:user] hash. However, if you don't carefully control which attributes are permitted, a malicious user could manipulate the params[:user] hash to set attributes that they shouldn't be able to access, such as is_admin or password_digest.

The Mass Assignment Vulnerability

Imagine your User model has attributes like name, email, password, and is_admin. You don't want ordinary users to be able to set the is_admin attribute, as this would allow them to grant themselves administrator privileges.

Without strong parameters, a malicious user could submit a form with the following parameters:

```
params = { user: { name: "Hacker", email:
"hacker@example.com", password: "password", is_admin: true }
}
```

If you then create a new User object using these parameters, the is_admin attribute would be set to true, granting the user administrator privileges.

Strong Parameters to the Rescue: Explicitly Permitting Attributes

Strong parameters solve this problem by requiring you to explicitly permit which attributes can be set on your model. Any attributes that are not explicitly permitted will be ignored.

To use strong parameters, you need to define a private method in your controller that whitelists the permitted attributes:

```
class UsersController < ApplicationController
  def create
    @user = User.new(user_params)

    if @user.save
```

```
    redirect_to @user
  else
    render :new
  end
end

private

def user_params
  params.require(:user).permit(:name, :email, :password,
:password_confirmation)
end
end
```

Let's break down this code:

- params.require(:user): This ensures that the params hash contains a key called user. If the user key is missing, it will raise an exception.
- permit(:name, :email, :password, :password_confirmation): This specifies that only the name, email, password, and password_confirmation attributes are permitted. Any other attributes that are submitted in the params hash will be ignored.

Now, even if a malicious user submits a form with the is_admin attribute set to true, it will be ignored because it's not included in the permit list.

Best Practices for Using Strong Parameters

- **Always Use Strong Parameters:** Make it a habit to always use strong parameters when creating or updating records in your models.
- **Be Explicit:** Be explicit about which attributes you permit. Don't use the permit! method, which allows all attributes to be set.
- **Group Parameters by Resource:** Group your parameters by resource in the params hash (e.g., params[:user], params[:article]). This makes your code more organized and easier to read.
- **Test Your Strong Parameters:** Write tests to ensure that your strong parameters are working correctly.

My "Security Scare" Story: I once worked on a Rails application that had a serious mass assignment vulnerability. A malicious user was able to manipulate the parameters and set the is_admin attribute on their account, granting themselves administrator privileges. It was a major security breach that could have had disastrous consequences. From that day forward, I became a strong advocate for using strong parameters and taking security seriously.

Key Takeaways:

- Mass assignment is a security vulnerability that allows malicious users to set unauthorized attributes on your models.
- Strong parameters protect your application from mass assignment vulnerabilities by requiring you to explicitly permit which attributes can be set.
- Always use strong parameters when creating or updating records in your models.

By mastering strong parameters, you'll be able to build more secure and reliable Rails applications that protect your data from malicious attacks.

9.4 Displaying Validation Errors: Guiding Users to Success

You've learned how to create models, generate forms, and protect your application from mass assignment vulnerabilities. Now, let's focus on providing a great user experience by displaying validation errors clearly and effectively.

Think of validation errors as friendly nudges that guide users to enter valid and consistent data. Clear and informative error messages can significantly improve the user experience and prevent frustration.

Why Display Validation Errors?

- **Improved User Experience:** Users need to know when they've entered invalid data so they can correct their mistakes.
- **Data Integrity:** Displaying validation errors helps ensure that only valid data is stored in your database.
- **Reduced Support Costs:** By providing clear error messages, you can reduce the number of support requests from users who are confused about how to use your application.

The errors Object: Your Error Information Hub

When a model fails validation (e.g., when you call .save), the errors object is populated with information about the validation failures. This errors object is an instance of ActiveModel::Errors and provides a set of methods for accessing the error messages.

Accessing Error Messages

Here are some useful methods for accessing error messages:

- errors.any?: Returns true if there are any errors, false otherwise.
- errors.messages: Returns a hash of error messages, where the keys are the attribute names and the values are arrays of error messages.
- errors[:attribute]: Returns an array of error messages for a specific attribute.
- errors.full_messages: Returns an array of human-readable error messages that include the attribute name (e.g., "Title can't be blank").

Displaying Error Messages in Your Views

The most common way to display validation errors in your views is to iterate over the errors.full_messages array and display each error message in a list.

Example: In the app/views/articles/new.html.erb view, you can display the validation errors like this:

```erb
<% if @article.errors.any? %>
  <div id="error_explanation">
    <h2><%= pluralize(@article.errors.count, "error") %>
prohibited this article from being saved:</h2>

    <ul>
      <% @article.errors.full_messages.each do |message| %>
        <li><%= message %></li>
      <% end %>
    </ul>
  </div>
<% end %>
```

Let's break down this code:

- <% if @article.errors.any? %>: This checks if there are any errors on the @article object.
- <div id="error_explanation">: This creates a div element with the ID error_explanation to contain the error messages. This ID is often used for styling the error messages.

- `<h2><%= pluralize(@article.errors.count, "error") %> prohibited this article from being saved:</h2>`: This displays a heading that indicates the number of errors. The pluralize helper automatically pluralizes the word "error" based on the number of errors.
- `<ul>`: This creates an unordered list to display the individual error messages.
- `<% @article.errors.full_messages.each do |message| %>`: This iterates over each error message in the errors.full_messages array.
- `<li><%= message %></li>`: This displays each error message in a list item.

With this, users can now read the various reasons why they were unable to save the data, improving the useability of the form!

Customizing Error Message Display

You can customize the way that validation errors are displayed in your views. For example, you can display error messages inline next to each form field:

```
    <div>
  <%= form.label :title %><br>
  <%= form.text_field :title %>
  <% if @article.errors[:title].any? %>
    <p class="error"><%= @article.errors[:title].first %></p>
  <% end %>
</div>
```

In this example, we're checking if there are any errors for the title attribute. If there are, we're displaying the first error message in a paragraph with the class error.

Here, we are just setting the first error, as listing the rest will result in making it too cluttered. Be sure to set it in a place that is easy to read and does not destroy the website's design.

Internationalizing Error Messages

Rails supports internationalization (i18n), which allows you to translate your application into different languages. You can also internationalize your validation error messages.

To internationalize a validation error message, you need to add an entry to your locale file (e.g., config/locales/en.yml). The entry should follow this format:

```
    en:
  errors:
    messages:
      blank: "can't be blank"
      too_short: "is too short (minimum is %{count}
characters)"
```

You can then use these keys in your model validations:

```
    validates :title, presence: true, length: { minimum: 5,
message: "is too short" }
```

With this, it shows how Rails handles error messages for all cases with a clean and neat syntax!

My "Error Encounter" Story: I once worked on a Rails application where the validation errors were displayed in a generic and unhelpful way. Users were constantly getting confused about what they were doing wrong and were submitting a lot of support requests. After improving the error message display, the number of support requests plummeted, and users were much happier.

Key Takeaways:

- Displaying validation errors is essential for providing a great user experience and ensuring data integrity.
- The errors object provides access to the validation error messages.
- You can iterate over the errors.full_messages array to display the error messages in a list.
- You can customize the way that validation errors are displayed in your views.
- Rails supports internationalization (i18n) for your validation error messages.

By mastering the art of displaying validation errors, you'll be able to create more user-friendly and reliable Rails applications that guide users to success.

9.5 File Uploads: Adding Media to Your Web App Canvas

You've mastered the basics of handling text-based data in forms. Now, let's add a new dimension to your web applications by implementing *file uploads*. File uploads allow users to upload images, documents, and other types of files to your server, opening up a world of possibilities for richer and more interactive applications.

Think of file uploads as expanding your canvas. Now you're no longer limited to just text and data, but rather, rich media, from jpegs, documents, videos, to audio, the sky is the limit.

Active Storage: Rails' Built-in File Management System

Rails provides a powerful and convenient way to handle file uploads called *Active Storage*. Active Storage simplifies the process of uploading files to cloud storage services like Amazon S3, Google Cloud Storage, or Microsoft Azure Storage, and it also provides support for local disk storage during development.

Setting Up Active Storage

Before you can use Active Storage, you need to install it.

1. **Install Active Storage:** Run the following command in your terminal:

   ```
   rails active_storage:install
   ```

   This will generate a migration file for creating the necessary tables for Active Storage.

2. **Run the Migration:** Run the migration to create the Active Storage tables in your database:

   ```
   rails db:migrate
   ```

Attaching Files to Your Model

To allow your model to accept file uploads, you need to add an attachment to your model using the has_one_attached or has_many_attached methods.

- has_one_attached: Use this for a one-to-one relationship (e.g., an article has one attached image).
- has_many_attached: Use this for a one-to-many relationship (e.g., an article has many attached images).

Example: Let's add a has_one_attached attachment to our Article model to allow users to upload an image for each article:

```
class Article < ApplicationRecord
  has_one_attached :image #This creates a one to one
relationship.
end
```

Now, your Article model has an image attachment that can be used to upload and store image files.

Displaying File Upload Fields in Your Forms

To allow users to upload files, you need to add a file_field to your form.

Example: In the app/views/articles/_form.html.erb partial, you can add a file_field like this:

```
<div>
<%= form.label :image %><br>
<%= form.file_field :image %>
</div>
```

This will generate an HTML file input field that allows users to select an image file to upload.

Processing the File Upload

In your controller, you need to permit the image attribute in your strong parameters:

```
private
```

```
def article_params #Method to set the properties that can be
edited for a specific object
  params.require(:article).permit(:title, :text, :image) #
Only allows the title and the text value to be set!
end
```

And you're set! Rails will automatically handle the file upload, storing the file in your configured storage service (e.g., Amazon S3) and creating a record in the active_storage_attachments table.

Displaying Uploaded Images

To display uploaded images in your views, you can use the image_tag helper, passing it the attachment object:

```
<%= image_tag @article.image %> #Shows the image for
the article
```

This will generate an HTML <img> tag with the correct URL for the uploaded image.

Image Transformations (Basic)

Active Storage allows you to perform basic image transformations, such as resizing and cropping, using the variant method.

Example: To display a thumbnail of the uploaded image, you can use the variant method to resize the image to a specific size:

```
<%= image_tag @article.image.variant(resize_to_limit:
[100, 100]) %>
```

This will generate a thumbnail of the image with a maximum width and height of 100 pixels.

You can set it for specific attributes or the general case by going to /config/storage.yml

Security Considerations

- **File Size Limits:** Set a maximum file size limit to prevent users from uploading excessively large files.
- **File Type Validation:** Validate the file type to ensure that users are only uploading allowed file types (e.g., images, documents).
- **Sanitize Filenames:** Sanitize filenames to prevent directory traversal attacks.
- **Secure Storage:** Use a secure storage service like Amazon S3 to store your uploaded files.

My "File Fumble" Story: I once worked on an application that didn't have proper file type validation in place. A malicious user was able to upload an executable file, which was then executed on the server, compromising the security of the entire application. I learned the hard way that file uploads can be a significant security risk if not handled carefully.

Key Takeaways:

- Active Storage simplifies the process of handling file uploads in Rails.
- Use has_one_attached or has_many_attached to add attachments to your models.
- Use the file_field helper to display file upload fields in your forms.
- Use the image_tag helper to display uploaded images in your views.
- Remember to add it to Strong Parameters!
- Implement security measures to protect your application from malicious uploads.

By mastering file uploads with Active Storage, you'll be able to create more engaging and feature-rich Rails applications that allow users to share and interact with files seamlessly.

Chapter 10: Model Associations: Connecting Your Data World

You've mastered the basics of creating models and storing data. Now, it's time to explore the relationships between your data. In the real world, data rarely exists in isolation. It's usually connected to other pieces of data in meaningful ways. The concept of data is what relational databases are designed around, after all!

Think of model associations as the glue that holds your data together. They allow you to define relationships between your models, making it easier to query, manage, and display related data. It allows your code to start resembling something like what you would see in the real world.

10.1 Understanding Database Relationships: Weaving the Web of Your Data

You've built models to represent individual entities in your application. Now, let's explore how those entities relate to each other. The relationships between your data are just as important as the data itself. For example, every blog post can have a user who posts them, or every book will have authors. Relational Databases are also build around this concept of relations!

Think of database relationships as your data's family tree. They define how different pieces of information are connected, allowing you to navigate your data and retrieve related information efficiently.

Why are Database Relationships Important?

- **Data Integrity:** Relationships ensure that your data is consistent and accurate.
- **Data Organization:** Relationships help you organize your data in a logical and meaningful way.
- **Query Efficiency:** Relationships allow you to retrieve related data quickly and efficiently.
- **Application Functionality:** Relationships enable you to build complex features that rely on the relationships between your data.

The Four Primary Types of Database Relationships

There are four primary types of database relationships that you'll encounter in most applications:

1. **One-to-Many (1:N):**
   - **Definition:** One record in one table is related to multiple records in another table.
   - **Example:** An author can write multiple articles. In this relationship, each author has *many* articles, and each article has *one* author.
   - **Implementation:**
     - The "many" side of the relationship (the articles table) has a foreign key column that references the "one" side of the relationship (the authors table). The foreign key column is typically named <singular_table_name>_id (e.g., author_id).
     - In the articles table, each row would have a single author_id that points to the id in the authors table.
   - **Real World Example:** One product can have many reviews.
2. **Many-to-One (N:1):**
   - **Definition:** Multiple records in one table are related to one record in another table.
   - **Relationship to One-to-Many:** This is simply the reverse perspective of the one-to-many relationship. If Author has one-to-many with Articles, then Articles has Many-to-one relationship with Author.
   - **Example:** Many articles are written by one author. In this relationship, each article has *one* author, and each author has *many* articles.
   - **Implementation:** The same as one-to-many, a table would point to another table.
   - **Real World Example:** Many employees work at one company.
3. **One-to-One (1:1):**
   - **Definition:** One record in one table is related to exactly one record in another table. This relationship is less common than one-to-many and many-to-one.
   - **Example:** A user has one profile. In this relationship, each user has *one* profile, and each profile belongs to *one* user.
   - **Implementation:** There are two ways to implement a one-to-one relationship:

- Option 1: The "one" side of the relationship (e.g., the users table) has a foreign key column that references the other table (e.g., the profiles table).
- Option 2: Both tables have foreign key columns that reference each other.
    - o **Real World Example:** A country has one capital.
4. **Many-to-Many (N:M):**
    - o **Definition:** Multiple records in one table can be related to multiple records in another table.
    - o **Example:** Articles and tags have many-to-many relationships. Articles can have multiple tags, and tags can be applied to multiple articles. This relationship involves a third table.
    - o **Implementation:** This relationship requires a *join table* (also known as a *through table* or *association table*) that connects the two tables.
        - The join table has two foreign key columns: one that references the primary key of the first table, and one that references the primary key of the second table.
        - Each row in the join table represents a relationship between one record from the first table and one record from the second table.
    - o **Real World Example:** Students taking many courses. Courses being taken by many students.

Visualizing Database Relationships

Database relationships can be visualized using diagrams. These diagrams help you understand the relationships between your data and can be useful for designing your database schema.

In a database diagram, tables are represented by boxes, and relationships are represented by lines connecting the boxes. The type of relationship is indicated by the symbols at the end of the lines:

- 1: One
- N: Many
- --: A relationship exists

For example, a one-to-many relationship between authors and articles would be represented like this:

```
Author   ---1:N---> Article
```

It would show that author has a 1 to many relationship to an article.

Importance of Understanding Database Relationships Before Coding

It is essential to understand your data before coding, so that you are able to write and scale effectively!

- Understand the business goals so that the database can be modeled effectively!
- Talk with the various stake holders so that you can model each table.

My "Relationship Revelation" Story: I used to think that databases were just a place to store raw data. But once I learned about database relationships, I realized that they were a powerful tool for organizing and connecting data in meaningful ways. It transformed the way I approached database design, and it allowed me to build more complex and feature-rich applications.

Key Takeaways:

- Database relationships define how different pieces of information are connected.
- The four primary types of database relationships are one-to-many, many-to-one, one-to-one, and many-to-many.
- Relationships are implemented using foreign keys and join tables.
- Visualizing database relationships with diagrams can be helpful for designing your database schema.

By understanding the principles of database relationships, you'll be able to design more effective and efficient database schemas for your Rails applications. This is a fundamental skill that will serve you well throughout your web development career.

10.2 Defining Associations: The Language of Relationships

You've learned the theory of database relationships. Now, let's put that knowledge into practice by exploring how to define those relationships within your Rails models. Defining the correct relationships with associations allow you to query and access all the data in a way that is readable and secure.

Think of model associations as the language that your models use to communicate with each other. They define the rules and syntax for expressing how your data is connected.

Rails' Association Methods: The Building Blocks

Rails provides a set of methods for defining associations between your models. These methods automatically generate the necessary code for managing the relationships between your data. The method you use will depend on the relationship that needs to be implemented:

- belongs_to: Establishes a one-to-one or many-to-one relationship.
- has_one: Establishes a one-to-one relationship.
- has_many: Establishes a one-to-many relationship.
- has_many :through: Establishes a many-to-many relationship.

belongs_to: Understanding the Single Connection

The belongs_to association is used to define a one-to-one or many-to-one relationship. It indicates that the model instance possesses a direct, single connection to another model. To see a working example, see the one with the author and article.

Key aspects of belongs_to:

- **Foreign Key:** The model that uses belongs_to will have a foreign key column that references the primary key of the associated model. This helps ensure there is always a valid object that the record will point to.
- **Singular Name:** The argument passed to belongs_to is the *singular* name of the associated model (e.g., author instead of authors).
- **Example Model:**

```
class Article < ApplicationRecord
  belongs_to :author #Creates a model to allow each article to have a foreign key of author_id
  validates :author, presence: true #Also ensures that there is an author
end
```

This allows articles to be bound to a singular author.

has_one: A Direct, Singular Link

The has_one association sets up a one-to-one connection with another model. In database terms, this model will have a single foreign key that is tied to the object.

Key aspects of has_one:

- **Foreign Key Placement:** The other model has a foreign key that refers back to the one declaring the has_one
- **Singular Name:** Similar to belongs_to, the argument is the *singular* form of the association's name
- **Example Code**

```
class Author < ApplicationRecord
  has_one :profile #Tells Rails that this object has a link
to a single profile
end
```

If you know that each author should always have a single profile, and want to ensure that the object exists and ties back to the right object, has one would be the way to go!

has_many: The Power of Collection

The has_many association defines a one-to-many relationship, meaning that a model has a collection of records of another model. In database terms, this model has a list of foreign keys that is associated with it.

Key aspects of has_many:

- **Plural Naming:** The name specified after has_many is plural, representing the other model that can exist
- **Referential Table:** In order to work, the other model needs to have the name of this model followed by _id that is used to refer to this model
- **Example Code**

```
class Author < ApplicationRecord
```

```
    has_many :articles  #Creates a relationship that the
author object has a has_many relationship to many articles
end
```

With this tag in place, you are able to call methods like author.articles

has_many :through: Connecting Many to Many

A many-to-many relationship is when two models can have multiple connections to each other, with the use of a joining model that is connected with two belongs_to tags to implement the relationship.

Key aspects of has_many through

- **Three Tables:** Needs to use the has_many on the first object, and the through model.
- **Join Table:** Needs to create a table to hold the foreign key. The foreign keys should be referenced on the other 2 resources. This will link the two objects together.
- **Multiple Associations:** As such, you must also make associations on each of the objects so they can pull information.
- **Example Code**

```
    # app/models/article.rb
class Article < ApplicationRecord
  has_many :article_tags #has many articletags
  has_many :tags, through: :article_tags #and each tag from
articletag
end

# app/models/tag.rb
class Tag < ApplicationRecord
  has_many :article_tags #has many articletags
  has_many :articles, through: :article_tags #and each
article from articletag
end

# app/models/article_tag.rb
class ArticleTag < ApplicationRecord
  belongs_to :article #Articletag belongs to a tag and
article
  belongs_to :tag
end
```

The most important part of this is the join model, as it is through that model that the other model will look at. Also, if you have attributes that are unique to the joining that should be saved, like a "position" or an "order", you'll need to have it placed here so you can keep track of any meta properties related to this connection.

Advanced Options: Customizing Associations

Rails provides a number of options for customizing associations, such as:

- class_name: Specifies the class name of the associated model. This is useful if the class name doesn't follow the Rails conventions.
- foreign_key: Specifies the name of the foreign key column. This is useful if the foreign key column doesn't follow the Rails conventions.
- dependent: Specifies what should happen when the associated object is destroyed. Common options are :destroy (destroy the associated objects) and :nullify (set the foreign key to nil).
- through: Specifies the join model to use for a has_many :through association.

My "Relationship" Reality Check Story: Initially, I relied on Rails to automatically infer all my relationships. It worked most of the time, but I often ran into subtle bugs and performance issues. Once I started explicitly defining my associations with the appropriate options, my code became much more robust and predictable.

Key Takeaways:

- Model associations define the relationships between your data.
- Rails provides methods for defining one-to-many (has_many, belongs_to), one-to-one (has_one, belongs_to), and many-to-many (has_many :through) relationships.
- Customizing association by specifying options helps add functionality to fit any relationship design that a model may have.

By understanding how to define model associations, you'll be able to create more complex and realistic data models that accurately represent the relationships between the entities in your application.

10.3 Working with Associated Data: Unleashing the Power of Relationships

You've successfully defined your model associations, mapping out the intricate web of connections between your data. Now, it's time to put those relationships to use! This section will explore how to access and manipulate associated data in your controllers and views, allowing you to build dynamic and interconnected user experiences.

Think of associated data as a treasure trove of information just waiting to be unlocked. Knowing how to access and display this data effectively will allow you to build richer and more engaging applications.

Accessing Associated Data in Your Controllers

In your controllers, you can use the associations you've defined to easily access related data.

Example: Let's say you have an Author model and an Article model with a one-to-many association (an author can have many articles). To retrieve all the articles written by a specific author, you can use the articles association:

```
class AuthorsController < ApplicationController
  def show #action to show
    @author = Author.find(params[:id]) #Find the single
author by id
    @articles = @author.articles #Find each article with this
author_id.
  end
end
```

Now the @articles array has an article list that you can work with.

The associated objects should also be accessible on the views by the same means.

Creating New Associated Objects

You can also use the associations to create new associated objects.

Example: Let's say you want to create a new article for a specific author. You can use the articles.build method to create a new Article object that is automatically associated with the author:

```
class ArticlesController < ApplicationController

  def create
    @article = @author.articles.new(article_params)

    respond_to do |format|
      if @article.save
        format.html { redirect_to @article, notice: "Article
was successfully created." }
        format.json { render :show, status: :created,
location: @article }
      else
        format.html { render :new, status:
:unprocessable_entity }
        format.json { render json: @article.errors, status:
:unprocessable_entity }
      end
    end
  end
end
```

Accessing Associated Data in Your Views

In your views, you can use the same associations to access related data. The main task is to get the correct data into the view first. Then you can use different operations to format the data for your end users.

Example: Let's say you want to display the name of the author for each article in the app/views/articles/index.html.erb view:

```
    <h1>Listing Articles</h1>

<ul>
  <% @articles.each do |article| %>
    <li>
      <h2><%= article.title %></h2>
      <p>By: <%= article.author.name %></p> #Gets the author
related to this article object
    </li>
  <% end %>
</ul>
```

Forming New Entries with Relationships

Forms can be set up that create a new database entry using the associations as a method.

To create a new entry with the author of an article:

1. First set the route as a resource
2. In that route specify the nesting resource, or the resources that can be performed under the route.

```
    resources :authors do
  resources :articles
end
```

If done correctly, then the forms will now create nested forms.

```
    <%= form_with(model: [@author, @article]) do |form| %>
```

IGNORE_WHEN_COPYING_START

And then you can generate all the links accordingly. With nested forms, the amount of information that can be displayed has expanded dramatically!

Common Pitfalls and How to Avoid Them

- **N+1 Queries:** This is a common performance issue that occurs when you're iterating over a collection of objects and accessing associated data in each iteration. This can result in a large number of database queries, which can significantly slow down your application.
    - **Solution:** Use eager loading to retrieve the associated data in a single query. You can use the includes method to eager load associations:

```
    @articles = Article.all.includes(:author) #Grabs each
of the authors from the database to prevent the N+1 problem.
```

- **Lazy Loading:** The anti-opposite of 1+N loading, but where the database loads over time. You are able to make some database connections faster, but the cost is that it would take an extraordinarily long time for a query to load. This could also affect code performance, as you may end up doing a lot of unecessary function calls without the correct data.

My "Aha Moment": Putting it All Together For a long time, model associations felt like an abstract concept. But once I started using them in my applications, I realized how powerful they were. I could easily access related data, build complex queries, and create dynamic user interfaces.

Key Takeaways:

- Associations allow you to access and manipulate related data in your controllers and views.
- Instance variables are used to pass associated data to your views.
- Eager loading is used to prevent N+1 queries.

By mastering working with associated data, you'll be able to build more complex, data driven, and engaging Rails applications.

10.4 Mastering Association Methods: Your Relational Toolkit

You've defined your model associations and explored how to access related data. Now, let's dive deeper into the specific methods that Rails provides for working with these relationships. These association methods are powerful tools that allow you to create, query, and manipulate associated data with ease.

Think of these methods as your specialized tools for working with your data's family tree. Each tool has a specific purpose, and mastering them will allow you to navigate and manage your relationships with precision and control.

Understanding Association Scopes

It's important to remember that when you call association methods, you are operating within the *scope* of the association. This means that the methods are applied to the *relationship* between the models, not just the models themselves.

The Essential Methods: Building, Creating, and Checking

Here are some of the most commonly used association methods:

- **association.build(attributes):** This method creates a new associated object *in memory*, but it does *not* save it to the database. This is useful for creating new objects that you want to customize before saving. It is important to note that attributes will need to be manually set when using this method.

```
@author = Author.find(1)  #Finds the first author
@article = @author.articles.build(title: "New Article", text:
"This is the content.") #Build the new model but does not
save

#Later
@article.save #Saves to the database
```

- **association.create(attributes):** This method creates a new associated object and *immediately* saves it to the database. This is a shortcut for calling build and then save. This method sets properties and tries to persist them right away.

```
@author = Author.find(1)
@article = @author.articles.create(title: "New Article",
text: "This is the content.") #Creates the object and tries
to persist it in one line.
```

- **association.exists?:** This method checks if there are any associated objects. It returns true if there are any associated objects, and false otherwise.

```
@author = Author.find(1)
if @author.articles.exists? #Checks that the object exists.
  puts "This author has articles"
else
  puts "This author has no articles"
end
```

You can also check for the existence of a specific associated object by passing its ID to the exists? method:

```
@author = Author.find(1)
if @author.articles.exists?(5)  # Check if author with ID 1
has an article with ID 5
```

```
    puts "The author has that article"
end
```

- **association.size:** This method returns the number of associated objects.

```
@author = Author.find(1)
puts "This author has #{@author.articles.size} articles"
#Prints out the author, and the count to the console.
```

- **association << object:** Adds another object to the relation. This adds another object to the relationship set for a certain relation.

```
@author = Author.find(1)
@tag = Tag.find(3)
@author.tags << @tag #This gives the author tag 3
```

Advanced Querying with Associations

You can use association methods to perform more complex queries on your associated data.

- **Chaining Methods:** You can chain association methods to build complex queries. For example, you can use the where method to filter the associated objects:

```
@author = Author.find(1)
@articles = @author.articles.where(published: true) #Only
load the article if published is true
```

- **Eager Loading with includes:** You can use includes to specify certain relationships to load. This will reduce the amount of queries being done and speed up the page.

```
@articles = Article.all.includes(:author)
```

My "Association Aha" Moments: At first, all the association methods felt like a bit of a jumble. But once I understood the underlying principles and how they related to the database schema, it all clicked into place. It's important to know your underlying models to use these different calls!

Key Takeaways:

- Rails provides a set of methods for working with model associations.
- These methods allow you to create, query, and manipulate associated data.
- Commonly used association methods include build, create, exists?, size, and includes and the proper query method.

By mastering these association methods, you'll be able to build more sophisticated and data-driven Rails applications with confidence.

Chapter 11: User Authentication and Authorization: Securing Your Application's Gates

You've learned how to build models, create views, and process data. Now, it's time to secure your application by implementing user authentication and authorization. These are essential security features that control who can access your application and what they can do.

Think of authentication and authorization as the gatekeepers of your application. They verify the identity of users and control their access to different resources. You'll often hear these terms abbreviated as AuthN (authentication) and AuthZ (authorization).

11.1 Authentication and Authorization: Guarding Your Application's Crown Jewels

You've learned how to build web applications, but have you considered the digital locks you need to put in place to protect them? Authentication and Authorization, often shortened to AuthN and AuthZ respectively, are the cornerstones of security in any web application. Without them, your application is essentially an open house, inviting anyone to come in and do whatever they please.

Think of authentication and authorization as the security system for your house. Authentication is like verifying that the person entering your house is who they say they are (e.g., by checking their ID). Authorization is like determining which rooms they are allowed to access (e.g., guests can access the living room and kitchen, but not the master bedroom).

Authentication: Verifying "Who Are You?"

Authentication is the process of verifying the identity of a user. It answers the question: "Who are you?" How do you know that the current user is John and not an imposter trying to take his identity?
It's very important to confirm that someone is who they are.

Key aspects of authentication:

- **Identification:** Identifying the user by their username, email address, or some other unique identifier.
- **Verification:** Verifying the user's identity by checking their password, security token, or other credentials.

Why is Authentication Important?

- **Data Protection:** You need to ensure that only authorized users can access sensitive data. For example, you don't want just anyone to be able to view other users' personal information.
- **Account Security:** You need to protect user accounts from unauthorized access. Without authentication, anyone could potentially take over someone else's account.
- **Compliance:** Many regulations, such as GDPR, require you to implement authentication to protect user data.

Authorization: Controlling "What Can You Do?"

Authorization is the process of determining what a user is allowed to do. It answers the question: "What are you allowed to do?"

Just knowing a user isn't enough, you also need to control what they can access and change. What if a regular user should only be able to create articles but not delete other people's articles?

Key aspects of authorization:

- **Roles:** Defining different roles for users (e.g., admin, editor, viewer).
- **Permissions:** Granting permissions to each role (e.g., admins can create, read, update, and delete articles; editors can create and update articles; viewers can only read articles).
- **Access Control:** Enforcing access control rules based on the user's role and permissions.

Why is Authorization Important?

- **Prevent Unauthorized Actions:** You need to prevent users from performing actions that they are not authorized to do. For example, you don't want ordinary users to be able to delete articles that belong to other users.

- **Maintain Data Integrity:** You need to ensure that only authorized users can modify data, preventing accidental or malicious data corruption.
- **Enforce Business Rules:** You can use authorization to enforce business rules that are specific to your application.

Real-World Analogy

Imagine a hospital:

- **Authentication:** The security guard at the entrance checks your ID to verify that you are who you say you are.
- **Authorization:** Your role (doctor, nurse, patient, visitor) determines which areas of the hospital you are allowed to access. Doctors can access patient records and operating rooms, while visitors can only access the waiting room and cafeteria.

Benefits of Robust Authentication and Authorization

- **Enhanced Security:** Protects your application from unauthorized access and data breaches.
- **Improved Data Integrity:** Ensures that only valid and authorized data is stored in your database.
- **Increased User Trust:** Users are more likely to trust your application if you have strong security measures in place.
- **Compliance with Regulations:** Helps you comply with data privacy regulations such as GDPR and HIPAA.
- **Scalability and Maintainability:** Makes it easier to manage user access as your application grows and evolves.

My "Security Wake-Up Call" Story: When I first started building web applications, I didn't fully appreciate the importance of authentication and authorization. I thought that as long as I had a password field on my login form, I was secure enough. Then I learned about the many ways that malicious users can bypass simple security measures and gain unauthorized access to sensitive data. That's when I realized that security had to be a top priority.

Key Takeaways:

- Authentication verifies the identity of a user ("Who are you?").

- Authorization determines what a user is allowed to do ("What can you do?").
- Authentication and authorization are essential for protecting your application from unauthorized access and data breaches.
- Robust authentication and authorization can lead to increased user trust, and compliance.

By understanding the importance of authentication and authorization, you'll be well-prepared to build secure and trustworthy Rails applications that protect your data and provide a safe and enjoyable experience for your users.

11.2 Implementing Authentication with Devise: The Easy Button for Secure Sign-In

You've learned why authentication is critical for protecting your application. Now, let's explore a powerful gem that simplifies the process of implementing authentication in Rails: **Devise**.

Think of Devise as your all-in-one authentication solution. It handles the complexities of user registration, login, password management, and more, allowing you to focus on building the core features of your application. It provides all the basic components of a password secured account.

Why Choose Devise?

- **Comprehensive Solution:** Devise provides a complete authentication solution, covering all the common authentication features.
- **Customizable:** Devise is highly customizable, allowing you to tailor it to your specific needs.
- **Secure:** Devise follows security best practices and helps you protect your application from common authentication-related vulnerabilities.
- **Easy to Use:** Devise is relatively easy to install and configure, even for beginners.
- **Active Community:** Devise has a large and active community, so you can find plenty of resources and support online.

Devise's Core Features

Devise provides the following core features:

- **User Registration:** Allows users to create new accounts.
- **Login and Logout:** Allows users to sign in and out of their accounts.
- **Password Reset:** Allows users to reset their passwords if they forget them.
- **Email Confirmation:** Requires users to confirm their email addresses before they can access their accounts.
- **Account Locking:** Locks accounts after a certain number of failed login attempts.
- **OAuth Authentication:** Supports authentication with third-party providers like Google, Facebook, and Twitter (using gems like omniauth-facebook).

Setting up Devise
The install process is relatively straightforward.

1. **Add Devise to your Gemfile:** Open your Gemfile and add the following line:

```
gem 'devise'
```

1. **Run bundle install:** To install devise use the following command

```
bundle install
```

1. **Set up devise in your project**: To set up the various things for your device, run

```
rails generate devise:install
```

This will set up devise in your project and require you to check for devise setup notes. Also change the config/environments/development.rb file with

```
config.action_mailer.default_url_options = { host: 'localhost', port: 3000 }
```

This is so devise can build the url for you.

1. **Creating a User model:** Now you have to create a user model and assign all the features to the model. You can use a base model or generate a model.

```
rails generate devise user
```

1. **Run the migrations:** Create and update the database according to these migrations.

```
rails db:migrate
```

These steps are all that is needed for you to implement the Devise authentication in your Rails 8 application. Next is customization!

Adding Devise Views to the Application (Optional)

If you want to customize the Devise views (e.g., to match the design of your application), you can run the following command:

```
rails generate devise:views
```

This will copy the Devise views to the app/views/devise/ directory, where you can modify them to your liking. These files define the HTML pages and functionality for you to see. They are set to inherit from the standard layouts of your pages.

Protecting Controller Actions with before_action

To ensure that only authenticated users can access certain controller actions, you can use the authenticate_user! method as a before_action filter.

Example: Let's say you want to require users to be logged in before they can create or edit articles. You can add the following code to your ArticlesController:

```
class ArticlesController < ApplicationController
  before_action :authenticate_user!, except: [:index, :show]
#Only allow the guest user to view the show and index
  # ...
end
```

- before_action :authenticate_user!: This tells Rails to call the authenticate_user! method before executing any of the actions in the controller.
- except: [:index, :show]: This specifies that the authenticate_user! filter should *not* be applied to the index and show actions, allowing anyone to view the list of articles and a specific article.

My "Devise Delight" Story: I used to dread implementing authentication in my Rails applications. It always seemed like a complex and time-consuming task. Then I discovered Devise, and it transformed the way I approached authentication. Devise made it incredibly easy to add authentication to my applications, and it handled all the nitty-gritty details for me.

Key Takeaways:

- Devise is a powerful gem that simplifies the process of implementing authentication in Rails.
- Devise provides a complete authentication solution, covering all the common authentication features.
- Use the authenticate_user! method to protect controller actions from unauthorized access.
- Customize the Devise views to match the design of your application.

By mastering Devise, you'll be able to add robust and secure authentication to your Rails applications with ease.

11.3 Implementing the Core: Registration, Login, and Logout with Devise

You've installed Devise, and you have a User model ready to go. Now, it's time to wire up the core functionality that allows users to create accounts, sign in, and sign out of your application. Devise makes this surprisingly easy, providing all the necessary routes, controllers, and views.

Think of these actions as setting up the welcome center, security check, and exit doors to your application. They define how users enter, interact with, and leave your digital space.

Default Routes: Devise's Automatic Setup

Devise automatically creates a set of routes for user authentication. You can see these routes by running the command rails routes in your terminal.

Key Devise Routes:

- **GET /users/sign_up:** Displays the user registration form.
- **POST /users:** Creates a new user account.
- **GET /users/sign_in:** Displays the user login form.
- **POST /users/sign_in:** Authenticates the user and signs them in.
- **DELETE /users/sign_out:** Signs the user out.
- **GET /users/password/new:** Displays the password reset request form.
- **POST /users/password:** Sends a password reset email to the user.
- GET /users/password/edit?reset_password_token=...: Displays the password reset form.
- PUT /users/password OR PATCH /users/password: Updates the user's password.

Displaying the Registration Form

To display the user registration form, you can create a link to the /users/sign_up URL in your view:

```
<%= link_to "Sign up", new_user_registration_path %>
#This builds a working sign-up form.
```

This will generate a link that takes the user to the Devise-generated registration form. On the page, users are able to input their email, password, and password verification.

Displaying the Login Form

To display the user login form, you can create a link to the /users/sign_in URL in your view:

```
<%= link_to "Log in", new_user_session_path %> #This
builds a working sign-in form.
```

This will generate a link that takes the user to the Devise-generated login form. On the page, users are able to input their email and password to sign in.

Adding a Logout Link

To add a logout link to your view, you can use the link_to helper with the destroy_user_session_path and set the method option to delete:

```
<%= link_to "Log out", destroy_user_session_path,
method: :delete %> #Link will log out the current user.
```

The method: :delete option tells Rails that the link should send a DELETE request to the server.

Checking if a User is Signed In

Devise provides a helper method called user_signed_in? that you can use in your views and controllers to check if a user is currently signed in.

```
<% if user_signed_in? %>
  <p>Welcome, <%= current_user.email %>!</p>
  <%= link_to "Log out", destroy_user_session_path, method:
:delete %>
<% else %>
  <%= link_to "Sign up", new_user_registration_path %>
  <%= link_to "Log in", new_user_session_path %>
<% end %>
```

This will display a welcome message and a logout link if the user is signed in, and it will display a sign-up link and a login link if the user is not signed in.

Accessing the Current User

Devise also provides a helper method called current_user that you can use in your views and controllers to access the currently signed-in user.

```
class ArticlesController < ApplicationController
before_action :authenticate_user!
def create
  @article = current_user.articles.new(article_params)
#Creates the current user and passes that to the article

  if @article.save
    redirect_to @article
  else
    render :new, status: :unprocessable_entity
```

196

```
        end
     end
  end
```

Customizing the Views (Optional)

As discussed in the previous section, you can customize the Devise views by running the command rails generate devise:views. This will copy the Devise views to the app/views/devise/ directory, where you can modify them to match the design of your application.

My "Authentication Activation" Story: I remember the satisfaction of successfully setting up user registration, login, and logout in my Rails application. It was a significant milestone that gave me a sense of accomplishment and confidence in my ability to build secure and functional web applications. The main thing that helps is just following the steps, it's almost easy to copy and paste the lines!

Key Takeaways:

- Devise automatically sets up the routes, controllers, and views for user registration, login, and logout.
- Use the link_to helper with the appropriate paths to generate links to the Devise-generated pages.
- Use the user_signed_in? helper method to check if a user is signed in.
- Use the current_user helper method to access the currently signed-in user.
- Customize the Devise views to match the design of your application.

By mastering these basic authentication features, you'll be well-prepared to build secure and user-friendly Rails applications.

11.4 Implementing Authorization: Building the Gates and Fences

You've successfully implemented authentication, verifying the identity of your users. Now, it's time to control what those users are *allowed* to do within your application. This is where *authorization* comes in.

Think of authorization as setting up the gates and fences that determine who can access which areas of your application. It's about enforcing rules and permissions to ensure that users can only perform actions that they are authorized to perform.

Authorization vs. Authentication: Understanding the Difference

It's important to understand the difference between authentication and authorization:

- **Authentication:** Verifies *who* the user is.
- **Authorization:** Determines *what* the user is allowed to do.

A user can be successfully authenticated (e.g., they have entered the correct username and password) but still not be authorized to perform a specific action (e.g., delete an article).

Implementing Authorization: A Step-by-Step Guide

There are several ways to implement authorization in Rails, ranging from simple manual checks to more complex solutions using gems like Pundit or CanCanCan. We'll start with a basic approach and then explore more advanced options.

1. Defining User Roles

The first step is to define the different roles that users can have in your application. Common roles include:

- admin: Has full access to all features.
- editor: Can create, update, and delete content.
- author: Can create and update their own content.
- viewer: Can only view content.

You can store the user's role in a database column (e.g., role in the users table). Alternatively, you can use a more complex system for managing roles and permissions.

Adding a role Attribute to the User Model:

The first step will be to generate a migration with a role column on the User, which will define the type of user it is.

```
rails g migration add_role_to_users role:integer
```

You also need to set a default, such as by opening your migration file.

```
class AddRoleToUsers < ActiveRecord::Migration[7.1]
  def change
    add_column :users, :role, :integer, default: 0
  end
end
```

Then in the model you can define these constants (or you can store as a string and then convert)

```
class User < ApplicationRecord
  enum role: {normal: 0, admin: 1}
end
```

2. Implementing Authorization Checks in Your Controllers

Once you have defined your roles, you can implement authorization checks in your controllers to restrict access to specific actions.

Let's create a few functions to help with authorization

```
def admin_only
  return unless current_user.admin? #Verifies it's the admin.

  redirect_to root_path, alert: 'Admins only.' #And return
end
```

This helper function checks for a given action, and makes sure they are part of the admin group. Another can also be made for the current user.

```
def correct_user
  @article = Article.find(params[:id]) #Uses this to find what
is the article the user wants to manipulate.

  return if @article.user == current_user #If they are,
continue with the method

  redirect_to root_path, alert: "This is not your article."
#Otherwise, fail
end
```

Adding to Actions

These actions are then added at the top so that it performs certain actions

```
before_action :admin_only, only: [:admin,
:anotheradminaction]
before_action :correct_user, only: [:update, :destroy]
```

This restricts the admin functions to the admin. And the update and destroy functions to the current user.

You can also put the conditions inline as well in the controller function. There are various ways to implement!

Using Gems for More Complex Authorization (e.g., Pundit, CanCanCan)

For more complex authorization requirements, you can use gems like Pundit or CanCanCan. These gems provide a more structured and flexible way to define authorization rules.

Key Takeaways for Authorization Gems:

- **Centralized Authorization Logic:** Helps you centralize authorization logic in policy objects, making your controllers cleaner and more maintainable.
- **Flexible Rules:** Allows you to define complex authorization rules that are based on the user's role, the resource being accessed, and the context of the request.
- **Easy to Test:** Makes it easier to test your authorization logic.

My "Access Denied" Story: I once worked on an application that had a poorly implemented authorization system. Users were able to access data that they shouldn't have been able to see, and it was difficult to track down and fix the vulnerabilities. That's when I realized that authorization was just as important as authentication and that it needed to be implemented carefully and consistently.

Key Takeaways:

- Authorization controls what users are allowed to do.

- You can implement authorization by defining user roles and implementing authorization checks in your controllers.
- Consider using gems like Pundit or CanCanCan for more complex authorization requirements.

By mastering authorization, you'll be able to build secure and trustworthy Rails applications that protect your data and enforce your application's business rules. You will need to make it user based, by having a good setup for knowing what each user can access.

11.5 Best Practices for Secure Authentication: Forging an Impenetrable Defense

You've implemented authentication, giving your application a basic level of security. However, simply having a username and password is not enough to protect your users and your data. You need to follow security best practices to minimize risks and ensure that your authentication system is as secure as possible.

Think of these best practices as building a fortress around your application's authentication system. Each layer of defense adds another level of protection, making it more difficult for attackers to breach your security.

Password Security: The Foundation of Trust

- **Use Strong Passwords:** The number one best practice is for users to create strong passwords. While you can't dictate what users decide to write, it is essential that the service should try to enforce some requirements for strength.
    - ○ **Enforce Minimum Length:** A minimum length of 12 characters is recommended.
    - ○ **Encourage Complexity:** Recommend a mix of uppercase letters, lowercase letters, numbers, and symbols.
- **Password Storage: Hash, Don't Store:** Never store passwords in plain text. Use a strong hashing algorithm, such as bcrypt, to store passwords. Bcrypt is a one-way hashing algorithm that is designed to be computationally expensive, making it difficult for attackers to crack passwords even if they gain access to the database. You will be using Bcrypt if you are using Devise.
- **Add Salt:** Salt is used to make brute force attacks more complicated.

Session Management: Secure Handling of Logged-In State

- **Use Secure Cookies:** Use secure cookies to store session information. Secure cookies are only transmitted over HTTPS, preventing them from being intercepted by attackers.
- **Set Cookie Expiration:** Set an expiration time for your cookies, so they aren't stored indefinitely.
- **Regenerate Session IDs:** Regenerate the session ID every time a user logs in or changes their password to prevent session fixation attacks.
- **Implement Session Timeout:** Automatically time out inactive sessions to prevent unauthorized access if a user leaves their computer unattended.

Protection Against Common Attacks

- **Brute-Force Attacks:** Implement rate limiting to prevent attackers from trying to guess passwords by making repeated login attempts. Rate limiting can be implemented using a gem like rack-attack.
- **Cross-Site Scripting (XSS):** Sanitize all user input before displaying it in your views to prevent attackers from injecting malicious JavaScript code into your web pages. Rails automatically escapes HTML entities by default, but you should always be vigilant about sanitizing user input.
- **Cross-Site Request Forgery (CSRF):** Use CSRF protection to prevent attackers from tricking users into performing actions they didn't intend to perform. Rails automatically provides CSRF protection, but you need to ensure that it is enabled and configured correctly.
- **SQL Injection:** Always use parameterized queries or ORM features to interact with the database. Avoid constructing SQL queries directly from user input, as this can create a SQL injection vulnerability. Rails Active Record protects against this by default if correctly implemented.

The Importance of HTTPS

Always use HTTPS to encrypt communication between the client and the server. HTTPS protects user data from being intercepted by attackers.

Implementing HTTPS is now easier than ever with services like Let's Encrypt, which provides free SSL/TLS certificates.

Multi-Factor Authentication (MFA): The Added Security Layer

Consider implementing multi-factor authentication (MFA) for added security. MFA requires users to provide two or more factors of authentication, such as something they know (password), something they have (security token), or something they are (biometric data).

MFA significantly reduces the risk of unauthorized access, even if an attacker manages to steal a user's password.

My "Security Obsession" Story: I used to think that security was someone else's problem. But then I realized that as a web developer, I had a responsibility to protect my users' data and privacy. That's when I became obsessed with security and started learning everything I could about authentication, authorization, and other security best practices.

Key Takeaways:

- Use strong passwords and store them securely.
- Implement secure session management practices.
- Protect against common attacks such as brute-force attacks, XSS, and CSRF.
- Always use HTTPS to encrypt communication between the client and the server.
- Consider implementing multi-factor authentication for added security.
- Follow security best practices throughout your development process.

By following these best practices, you'll be able to build more secure and trustworthy Rails applications that protect your users and their data. Make security a priority from the very beginning, and you'll be well-prepared to defend against the ever-evolving threats in the digital world.

Chapter 12: Testing: Your Safety Net and Quality Assurance Tool

You've learned how to build models, create views, and handle user requests. Now, it's time to ensure that your application is working correctly by writing tests. Testing is an essential part of the software development process that helps you catch bugs early, improve code quality, and reduce the risk of unexpected errors.

Think of testing as building a safety net for your application. It catches you when you make mistakes and helps you avoid costly accidents down the road. This also acts as a method of quality assurance to ensure that all functions of the code is working correctly before you hand it off to the end users.

12.1 Introduction to Testing in Rails: Cultivating a Culture of Code Quality

You've learned the core skills for building Rails applications. Now, it's time to learn how to ensure that your applications *work* reliably and predictably. Testing, is used to show that what is being done is functioning correctly!

Think of testing as cultivating a culture of quality within your development process. It's about instilling a mindset that values correctness, robustness, and maintainability.

Why Testing is Often Overlooked (Especially by Beginners)

It's understandable that testing can seem daunting or even unnecessary, especially when you're just starting out. Common reasons for skipping tests include:

- **Time Pressure:** "I don't have time to write tests. I just need to get the feature done!"
- **Complexity:** "Testing seems too complicated. I don't know where to start."
- **Lack of Immediate Gratification:** "Writing tests doesn't produce visible results like building features."

- **False Sense of Confidence:** "My code works perfectly, so I don't need tests." (Spoiler alert: it probably doesn't).

However, these are short-sighted reasons. While testing does require an initial investment of time and effort, it pays off handsomely in the long run.

The Benefits of a Testing Mindset: Building a Foundation for Success

Adopting a testing mindset from the very beginning of your development process offers numerous benefits:

- **Early Bug Detection:** Tests help you catch bugs early, before they make it into production. This can save you countless hours of debugging and prevent costly errors.
- **Reduced Debugging Time:** With adequate test coverage, it will help drastically cut down the amount of time to debug something. This gives more time to be spent on building out the code.
- **Improved Code Quality:** Writing tests forces you to think about the design of your code and how it should behave. This can lead to better code quality, more modular designs, and increased reusability.
- **Prevention of Regressions:** Tests help prevent regressions, which are bugs that are introduced when you make changes to existing code. Regression tests ensure that existing functionality continues to work as expected after you make changes.
- **Increased Confidence in Code Changes:** Before deploying changes you can ensure that the test suites are all working.
- **Documentation:** Tests can serve as documentation, demonstrating how your code is intended to be used. This makes it easier for other developers to understand your code and contribute to your project. This may include yourself.

Different Types of Tests: A Testing Toolbox

Rails provides several types of tests to cover different aspects of your application:

- **Unit Tests:** Test individual units of code, such as models, helpers, and mailers. They operate in isolation, mocking or stubbing out any dependencies to focus on testing a single piece of code.

  This helps when trying to find exactly what is the source of the bug.

- **Integration Tests:** Test the interaction between multiple components of your application, such as the interaction between a controller and a model. Integration tests provide more comprehensive coverage than unit tests but are also slower to run.

  This helps when you want to test the general workflow that all of these services go through.

- **System Tests:** Simulate user interaction with your application, testing the end-to-end functionality of your application. System tests are the slowest type of test but provide the highest level of confidence that your application is working correctly.

  This helps test the entire end flow of the project.

Testing Frameworks: Minitest vs. RSpec (A Brief Overview)

Rails supports two popular testing frameworks:

- **Minitest:** Is the default testing framework and is more lightweight.
- **RSpec:** Is more feature rich and used in most complex projects.

Both frameworks are excellent choices, and the choice often comes down to personal preference. This book will discuss both options that can be used!

Setting Up Testing Environment for Rails

When generating a new Rails application, you'll notice a test/ directory in the top-level directory. This directory is the home for all your tests. Inside test/, you'll find subdirectories for different types of tests:

- test/models/: Unit tests for your models.
- test/controllers/: Integration tests for your controllers.
- test/system/: System tests for your application.
- test/fixtures/: Sample data for your tests.
- test/test_helper.rb: A configuration file for your tests.

This file will provide you with what will be in use for testing.

My "Testing Skeptic" to "Testing Evangelist" Transformation: I didn't appreciate the value of testing until I experienced the pain of debugging a complex application without any tests. It was like trying to find a needle in a haystack. Now, I'm a firm believer in testing, and I make it a priority on every project I work on.

Key Takeaways:

- Testing is an essential part of the software development process.
- Adopting a testing mindset from the beginning can lead to better code quality, fewer bugs, and increased confidence.
- Rails provides three main types of tests: unit tests, integration tests, and system tests.
- You can use Minitest (the default) or RSpec for testing.

By embracing a culture of quality and making testing a priority, you'll be well-prepared to build robust, reliable, and maintainable Rails applications that provide a great user experience. And this point is what will make you a successful programmer!

12.2 Test-Driven Development (TDD): Inverting the Process for Powerful Results

You've learned why testing is important, but what if I told you that you could make testing even more effective by changing the order in which you write your code? That's the core idea behind **Test-Driven Development (TDD)**.

Think of TDD as inverting the traditional development process. Instead of writing the code first and then writing tests to verify it, you write the tests *first*. This seemingly simple change can have a profound impact on the quality, design, and maintainability of your code. TDD flips everything on its head by first thinking about the test cases before building what is being tested.

The TDD Cycle: Red-Green-Refactor

TDD follows a simple, iterative cycle known as "Red-Green-Refactor":

1. **Red:** Write a test that specifies the desired behavior of your code. This test should fail initially because you haven't implemented the code yet. It can be a unit, system, or integration test.

2. **Green:** Write the minimum amount of code necessary to make the test pass. The goal is to get the test to pass as quickly as possible, without worrying about code quality or design.
3. **Refactor:** Refactor your code to improve its design, readability, and maintainability. You can refactor with confidence because you have a test that verifies that your code is still working correctly. The last thing you should do it rewrite.

This cycle is repeated for each new feature or functionality that you add to your application.

Detailed Look

Let's break that down a little further.

Example: Creating a Model Method

Let's look at an example for a user model where we want to test a method called name_display that if the name attribute is nil, defaults to their email

- In test/models/user_test.rb you would put:

```
test "If name is not present display the email" do
@user.name - nil
assert_equal @user.email, @user.name_display
end
```

If this file does not exist you will have to generate it:

```
rails generate test_unit:model user
```

- We now want to implement that name in the app/models/user.rb code

```
def name_display
return self.name if self.name

self.email
end
```

- This is the minimum code that it takes to make the action run. If you run the test command with bin/rails test you will see that it passes!

- Last, look at the code again to see if you are able to improve the structure or any other small issues.

With that 3 step system, TDD allows you to create a method and code that has been verified to run.

Benefits of Test-Driven Development

- **Improved Code Quality:** TDD forces you to think about the design of your code before you implement it, leading to better code quality and more modular designs.
- **Reduced Bug Count:** TDD helps you catch bugs early in the development process, before they make it into production.
- **Increased Test Coverage:** TDD naturally leads to higher test coverage, as you are writing tests for every piece of code that you write.
- **Clearer Requirements:** Writing tests before code helps you clarify the requirements for each feature.
- **Confidence in Refactoring:** TDD gives you the confidence to refactor your code without fear of introducing regressions.
- **Documentation:** Tests serve as a form of living documentation, showing how your code is intended to be used.

Challenges of Test-Driven Development

- **Learning Curve:** TDD can take some time to learn and get used to. It requires a different way of thinking about development.
- **Initial Time Investment:** TDD requires an initial investment of time to write the tests before you write the code. However, this investment is usually offset by the reduced debugging time and improved code quality.
- **Over-Testing:** It's possible to over-test your code, writing tests that are too specific or that test implementation details rather than behavior.

My "TDD Transformation" Story: When I first heard about TDD, I thought it sounded crazy. Why would I write tests before I write the code? But as I started to practice TDD, I realized how powerful it was. It forced me to think about the design of my code before I implemented it, leading to better code quality and fewer bugs.

Key Takeaways:

- TDD is a development process where you write the tests before you write the code.
- The TDD cycle is Red-Green-Refactor.
- TDD can lead to improved code quality, reduced bug count, increased test coverage, clearer requirements, and confidence in refactoring.

By embracing TDD principles, you'll be able to write more robust, reliable, and maintainable Rails applications. It's a skill that will set you apart from other developers and make you a valuable asset to any team.

12.3 Your Testing Arsenal: Unit, Integration, and System Tests Unveiled

You've learned the principles of Test-Driven Development. Now, it's time to arm yourself with the knowledge and skills to write effective tests that cover all aspects of your Rails applications. Rails follows a design for its different tests, so each aspect is more simple to understand.

Each part plays a different role in the process of verifying what is being developed, so it's important to understand the differences between them:

- **Unit Tests:** Isolate and test individual components.
- **Integration Tests:** Checks connections between models, data, or properties.
- **System Tests:** Simulates User Experiences.

Understanding the Testing Pyramid

A good way to think about the different types of tests is to visualize them as a pyramid:

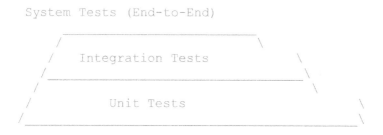

- The base of the pyramid consists of unit tests, which are the most numerous and the fastest to run.
- The middle layer consists of integration tests, which are fewer in number and slower to run than unit tests.
- The top of the pyramid consists of system tests, which are the fewest in number and the slowest to run.

The goal is to have a balanced testing strategy that covers all aspects of your application without relying too heavily on any one type of test. With too few different tests, it will result in errors happening down the line.

Unit Tests: Isolating the Parts

Unit tests are designed to test individual units of code in isolation. This means that you should mock or stub out any dependencies that the unit of code relies on. Unit tests are typically used to test:

- Models: Test model validations, methods, and business logic.
- Helpers: Test helper methods that format data or generate HTML.
- Mailers: Test that emails are being sent correctly.

Unit tests are fast and easy to write, making them ideal for catching bugs early in the development process. You should aim to have the most coverage in the unit test.

Example: Let's write a unit test for the Article model to ensure that the title attribute is required and has a minimum length of 5 characters:

```
require 'test_helper' #Loads standard settings for
Rails

class ArticleTest < ActiveSupport::TestCase #Inherits from
Test to implement

  def setup #Function to quickly set and load standard
properties.
    @article = Article.new
  end

  test "title must be present" do
    @article.text = "Some text" #Title is missing
    assert_not @article.valid? #Check to ensure the save was
not valid. Does the opposite of assert.
  end
```

```
test "title must be at least 5 characters long" do
    @article.title = "hi" #Too short of a title
    @article.text = "Some text" #Missing
    assert_not @article.valid? #Check to ensure the save was
not valid
  end
end
```

Key Points:

- require 'test_helper': Loads the test helper, which provides access to testing utilities and configurations.
- class ArticleTest < ActiveSupport::TestCase: Defines a test class that inherits from ActiveSupport::TestCase.
- test "title must be present" do ... end: Defines a test method that checks if the title attribute is required.
- article = Article.new(text: "Some text"): Creates a new Article object with the text attribute set. The title attribute is not set, so the validation should fail.
- assert_not article.valid?: Asserts that the article object is not valid. This means that the validation should have failed.
- assert_equal: Tests if the thing on the left is the same as the thing on the right.
- assert_match: Tests if the left and right are equal and that the thing on the right is a regex.

Integration Tests: The Connections

Integration tests are designed to test the interaction between multiple components of your application. This could be the interaction between a controller and a model, the interaction between two models, or the interaction between a view and a controller.

Integration tests are slower than unit tests but provide more comprehensive coverage. They are used to test that the different parts of your application are working together correctly.

Example: Let's write an integration test to ensure that users can create a new article:

1. In testing, you can either test to see if a model exists, or you can use a fixture

2. Create a fixture

```
    # In test/fixtures/articles.yml
one:
  title: "MyText"
  text: "MyText"

two:
  title: "MyText"
  text: "MyText"
```

1. Write an integration test (name whatever test you want, but in the form <model>_integration_test.rb)

```
    require "test_helper"

class Articles::IntegrationsTest <
ActionDispatch::IntegrationTest
  include Devise::Test::IntegrationHelpers

  setup do
    @user = users(:one) #Create a user fixture.
    sign_in @user #Login the user.
  end

  test "Creating a new article" do # Test name
    get new_article_path #First get the new_article_path to
load

    assert_response :success #assert it loads
    post articles_path,
        params: { article: { title: "Hello", text: "world!"
} } # create article with parameters
    assert_response :redirect #Check for proper link

    follow_redirect! #Load the page you want
    assert_response :success
    assert_select "p", text: "Title:\nHello" #Check it
renders the results on the webpage.
  end
end
```

Key Points:

- Test what happens end to end: you can chain a number of actions together using this.

213

System Tests: The User's Perspective

System tests are designed to simulate user interaction with your application, testing the end-to-end functionality of your application. System tests use a real web browser to interact with your application, allowing you to test the entire user experience. They require some testing for the overall flow, and that all properties or data are being properly used.

Example: Let's write a system test to ensure that users can create a new article:

```
require "application_system_test_case"

class ArticlesTest < ApplicationSystemTestCase
  test "Creating a new article" do #This is what the
description will read

    visit articles_path #Visit the model

    click_on "New article" #Select the new action

    fill_in "Title", with: "Creating a New Article" #Assign
to the properties using fill_in
    fill_in "Text", with: "Created the text!"

    click_on "Create Article"  #Press to create

    assert_text "Creating a New Article"  #Ensure the new
article is working
  end
end
```

Key Points:

- visit articles_path: Visits the articles page.
- click_on "New article": Clicks the "New article" link.
- fill_in "Title", with: "Creating a New Article": Fills in the "Title" field with the value "Creating a New Article".
- fill_in "Text", with: "Created the text!": Fills in the "Text" field with the value "Created the text!".
- click_on "Create Article": Clicks the "Create Article" button.
- assert_text "Creating a New Article": Asserts that the page contains the text "Creating a New Article".

My "Testing Epiphany" Story: I used to think that system tests were too slow and cumbersome to be worth the effort. But then I realized that they were the only way to truly test the end-to-end functionality of my application and ensure that everything was working correctly from the user's perspective.

Key Takeaways:

- Unit tests, integration tests, and system tests each have their own strengths and weaknesses.
- A well-rounded testing strategy should include all three types of tests.
- Unit tests are fast and easy to write, making them ideal for catching bugs early.
- Integration tests provide more comprehensive coverage by testing the interaction between multiple components.
- System tests simulate user interaction with your application, providing the highest level of confidence that everything is working correctly from the user's perspective.

By mastering these three types of tests, you'll be able to build more robust, reliable, and maintainable Rails applications that provide a great user experience.

12.4 RSpec vs. Minitest: Choosing Your Testing Sidekick

You've committed to writing tests (excellent!). Now comes another choice: which testing framework should you use? The two main contenders in the Rails world are **RSpec** and **Minitest**. Both are great choices, and the "best" one really depends on your personal style, project requirements, and team preferences. In practice, some projects use both in their code to utilize each tool, but it is more common to pick just one for easier use.

Think of RSpec and Minitest as different tool sets. One is more comprehensive, with the other that is basic and easy to learn.

Minitest: The Rails Default - Simple and Direct

Minitest is the default testing framework for Rails. It's a simple, lightweight, and easy-to-learn framework that is well-suited for beginners. The code that it provides is easier to read.

Key characteristics of Minitest:

- **Part of Ruby Standard Library:** Minitest is included in the Ruby standard library, so you don't need to install any additional gems to use it.
- **Simple and Direct:** Minitest has a straightforward and easy-to-understand API. It follows a simple convention-based approach to testing.
- **Focus on Assertions:** Minitest primarily focuses on assertions, which are used to check if a condition is true or false.
- **Good for Simple Tests:** Minitest is well-suited for writing simple unit tests and integration tests.

Example: A Minitest unit test for the Article model might look like this:

```
require "test_helper"

class ArticleTest < ActiveSupport::TestCase
  def setup
    @article = Article.new(title: "Sample Title", text:
"Sample Text")
  end

  test "title must be present" do
    @article.title = nil #Removes attribute
    assert_not @article.valid? # and validates it
  end

  test "Valid data works!" do
    assert @article.valid? #See if valid is valid
  end
end
```

Key points:

- require "test_helper": Loads the test helper, which provides access to testing utilities and configurations.
- class ArticleTest < ActiveSupport::TestCase: Defines a test class that inherits from ActiveSupport::TestCase.
- def test "title must be present" do ... end: Defines a test method that checks if the title attribute is required.
- assert_not @article.valid?: Asserts that the @article object is not valid.

RSpec: Expressive and Feature-Rich - For More Complex Scenarios

RSpec is a popular alternative testing framework for Ruby. It's a more expressive and feature-rich framework that provides a domain-specific language (DSL) for writing tests.

Key characteristics of RSpec:

- **Expressive DSL:** RSpec provides a more expressive and readable DSL for writing tests. This makes your tests easier to understand and maintain.
- **Focus on Behavior:** RSpec focuses on testing the *behavior* of your code, rather than the implementation details. This leads to more robust and maintainable tests.
- **Matchers:** RSpec provides a rich set of matchers that allow you to express your expectations in a clear and concise way.
- **Flexible:** RSpec is highly flexible and can be customized to fit your specific needs.
- RSpec can describe data and situations that are hard to implement with tests like Minitest.

Example: An RSpec unit test for the Article model might look like this:

```
    require 'rails_helper' #Now has access to all rails
methods.

RSpec.describe Article, type: :model do #Describes and names
the test group

  it "is not valid without a title" do # Describes the
function and names it
    article = Article.new(title: nil, text: "Some text")
#Makes sure we create new object

    expect(article).to_not be_valid #Checks that it does not
validate
  end

    it "is valid with valid values" do
    article = Article.new(title: "Title", text: "Some text")
#Makes sure we create new object

    expect(article).to be_valid #Checks that it does validate
  end
end
```

Key points:

- require 'rails_helper': Loads the Rails helper, which provides access to testing utilities and configurations.
- RSpec.describe Article, type: :model do ... end: Defines a test suite for the Article model. The type: :model option tells RSpec that this is a model test.
- it "is not valid without a title" do ... end: Defines a test example that checks if the title attribute is required.
- expect(article).to_not be_valid: Asserts that the article object is not valid.

Key Differences: A Quick Comparison

Feature	Minitest	RSpec
Syntax	Simple, direct, and Ruby-like	Expressive DSL with matchers
Focus	Assertions	Behavior
Extensibility	Limited	Highly extensible
Community Support	Good, but smaller than RSpec	Large and active community
Learning Curve	Easy to learn, especially for Ruby beginners	Steeper learning curve, but worth it for more complex projects
Default in Rails	Yes	No (requires installation)
Speed	Can be faster in certain test examples	Slower test suites may require tuning, but also more flexible

Choosing the Right Framework: A Matter of Preference

Ultimately, the choice between RSpec and Minitest comes down to personal preference and project requirements.

- **Choose Minitest if:**
  - You're new to testing and want a simple and easy-to-learn framework.
  - You prefer a more Ruby-like syntax.
  - You're working on a small or simple project.
- **Choose RSpec if:**
  - You want a more expressive and readable testing language.
  - You prefer to focus on testing the behavior of your code rather than the implementation details.
  - You're working on a larger or more complex project.

      o   You want use code constructs that do not exist in Minitest.

Migrating from Minitest to RSpec (Optional)

If you decide to switch from Minitest to RSpec after you've already started your project, you can use the rails generate rspec:install command to install RSpec and generate the necessary configuration files.

You'll then need to convert your existing Minitest tests to RSpec tests. This can be a time-consuming process, but it can be worth it if you prefer the RSpec DSL.

My "Testing Tribe" Story: I've used both Minitest and RSpec on different projects, and I've found that both frameworks have their strengths and weaknesses. Ultimately, the best choice is the one that you and your team are most comfortable with and that helps you write effective and maintainable tests.

Key Takeaways:

- RSpec and Minitest are two popular testing frameworks for Ruby and Rails.
- Minitest is the default testing framework for Rails and is simple and easy to learn.
- RSpec is a more expressive and feature-rich testing framework.
- The choice between RSpec and Minitest depends on personal preference and project requirements.

By understanding the strengths and weaknesses of each framework, you'll be able to make an informed decision about which one is right for you and your projects.

12.5 Testing Best Practices: Ascending to Testing Mastery

You've learned the fundamentals of testing and have chosen your testing framework. Now, it's time to elevate your testing skills and adopt a set of best practices that will help you write more effective, maintainable, and valuable tests. Learning the nuances on how to best test something will improve your ability to work with more difficult problems.

Think of these best practices as ascending to a higher level of testing mastery. It's about moving beyond just writing tests to writing *great* tests that provide real value and protect your application from bugs.

1. Write Tests for Everything (Aim for Near-Complete Coverage)

The most important best practice is to write tests for *all* of your code. This includes models, controllers, helpers, mailers, and any other custom code that you write. While achieving 100% test coverage is not always realistic or necessary, you should aim for near-complete coverage to ensure that all parts of your application are thoroughly tested. It is important to ensure there is test coverage, since tests need to be written for regressions and bugs.

This covers the various aspects from each point in the code.

2. Keep Tests Small and Focused (Single Responsibility Principle)

Each test should test a single unit of code or a single aspect of its behavior. This makes it easier to understand what the test is doing and to identify the source of any failures. It also helps avoid writing too much boilerplate code.

"Make sure each test does a single thing" is something that you will often hear because it allows developers to make assumptions of their code.

3. Use Descriptive Test Names (Clarity is Key)

Give your tests descriptive names that clearly indicate what they are testing. This makes it easier to understand the purpose of each test and to quickly identify the source of any failures. Naming convention usually goes as: does_something_for_a_certain_action

4. Follow the AAA Pattern (Arrange, Act, Assert)

Structure your tests using the Arrange-Act-Assert (AAA) pattern:

- **Arrange:** Set up the test environment, including creating any necessary objects or data.
- **Act:** Execute the code that you want to test.
- **Assert:** Verify that the code behaved as expected by making assertions about the results.

This is used to ensure that each test is doing exactly what it is meant to be doing!

5. Test with Correct Data vs. Edge Cases (Check All Scenarios)

When testing with different types of scenarios to be sure that you are not breaking any assumptions and that the code does what you expected.

These cases may include:

- Adding wrong data. If you expect a string and it needs a number.
- Inputting the wrong length. String length exceeds limits.
- Nil or blank values.

These should also have their own tests as well!

6. Use Test Doubles (Isolate Dependencies)

Test doubles (also known as mocks, stubs, and spies) are used to isolate your code from external dependencies. This allows you to test your code in isolation, without relying on external systems or databases.

It might be useful to do this when:

- Testing against the database
- Sending API requests
- Complex and time-consuming setup tasks

7. Run Tests Frequently (Early and Often)

Run your tests frequently to catch bugs early. You should run your tests every time you make a change to your code.

You can run all your tests using the rails test command:

```
rails test
```

You can run a specific test file by specifying the path to the file:

```
rails test test/models/article_test.rb
```

You can run a specific test method by specifying the method name:

```
rails test test/models/article_test.rb -n
test_title_must_be_present
```

8. Integrate Testing into Your Workflow (Continuous Integration)

Integrate testing into your development workflow using tools like continuous integration (CI). CI systems automatically run your tests every time you push code to a repository, providing you with immediate feedback on the quality of your code. If the tests fail, the application would not deploy to the server. Some examples of these testings are Travis CI, CircleCi, or Github Actions.

9. Write Tests for Bug Fixes (Prevent Regressions)

Whenever you fix a bug, write a test that reproduces the bug. This will help prevent the bug from reoccurring in the future.

10. Test Behavior, Not Implementation (Focus on the "What," Not the "How")

Focus on testing the *behavior* of your code, rather than the *implementation details*. This means that your tests should verify that your code is producing the correct output, regardless of how it is implemented. Test what it is doing, not how it is doing it.

By following these best practices, you'll be able to build more robust, reliable, and maintainable Rails applications that provide a great user experience.

My "Testing Wisdom" Story: Over time, I have worked on projects that test only a small percent and it has often been my task to add to the test suite. I have found that as tests get added, the amount of support tickets needed falls, giving users what they want! After a while, I became obsessed with writing clean, well-organized, and effective tests that truly protected my application from bugs and regressions.

Key Takeaways:

- Write tests for everything.
- Keep tests small and focused.

- Use descriptive test names.
- Follow the AAA pattern (Arrange, Act, Assert).
- Run tests frequently.
- Integrate testing into your workflow.
- Write tests for bug fixes.
- Test behavior, not implementation.

By embracing these testing best practices, you'll be able to create a culture of quality within your development process and build Rails applications that are both robust and enjoyable to use. Testing has the power to transform code from barely functioning to well maintained. Make sure to test everything!

Chapter 13: Rails 8 and Beyond: Modern Features and Timeless Best Practices

You've mastered the core concepts of Rails development. Now, it's time to explore the exciting new features and best practices that will help you build cutting-edge Rails 8 applications. The key to the new Rails is the focus on making it easy to make interactive apps, so we'll touch on that specifically with Turbo and Hotwire. This chapter also covers things that are always good to know to assist in scalability and maintainability!

Think of this chapter as your guide to building the "Rails of the Future," leveraging the latest tools and techniques to create applications that are both powerful and elegant.

13.1 Action Text: Unleash the Power of Rich Text Editing with Ease

You've conquered the basics of working with forms and text data in your Rails applications. Now, let's unlock a whole new level of content creation with **Action Text**. With standard data you can only accept basic text. But with rich text you can upload photos and other styled text that you would see in programs like Word!

Think of Action Text as your magic wand for transforming plain text areas into full-fledged rich text editors. It simplifies the process of creating and managing rich text content with attachments (e.g., images, videos) in your Rails applications, without the hassle of setting up a complex external solution.

What Is Action Text?

Action Text brings first-class rich text editing and storage capabilities directly into Rails. It's a powerful and elegant solution that simplifies the process of creating and managing rich text content with attachments (e.g., images, videos) using a WYSIWYG editor like Trix. Now, your users are only limited by their creativity, nothing else!

Why Use Action Text?

- **Seamless Integration:** Action Text seamlessly integrates with your Rails models and views, making it easy to add rich text editing to your existing applications.
- **WYSIWYG Editor:** Action Text uses the Trix editor, which provides a user-friendly WYSIWYG (What You See Is What You Get) interface for creating and editing rich text content.
- **Attachment Support:** Action Text allows you to easily upload and embed images, videos, and other attachments in your rich text content.
- **Clean HTML Output:** Action Text generates clean and well-structured HTML code that is easy to style and maintain.

Getting Started with Action Text: Installation and Setup

1. **Install Action Text:** Open your terminal and run the following command:

```
rails action_text:install
```

This will generate a migration file for creating the necessary tables for Action Text and install the Trix editor.

2. **Run the Migration:** Run the migration to create the Active Text tables in your database:

```
rails db:migrate
```

This command will set up what is used to attach rich text objects to the current model.
Active Storage is what allows images to be attached.

Adding Rich Text Content to Your Model

To add rich text content to your model, you need to use the has_rich_text macro.

Example: Let's add rich text content to our Article model:

```
class Article < ApplicationRecord
  has_rich_text :content  #Creates the rich text
end
```

This tells Rails that the Article model has a rich text attribute called content.

That command also sets up the necessary calls to the database in the back end. By default, Action Text makes use of Active Storage to store any assets that are created.

Displaying the Rich Text Editor in Your Forms

To display the rich text editor in your forms, you can use the rich_text_area helper:

```
<%= form.rich_text_area :content %> #Displays the area
for the users to input.
```

NOTE: You'll still need the standard form_with call described previously to implement this!

This will generate a Trix editor that allows users to create and edit rich text content. You also must permit this object on the controller to ensure that the property can be accessed and that it's safe to use:

```
def article_params
  params.require(:article).permit(:title, :text, :image,
:content)
end
```

Now you are able to save the form, and you now have a way for users to input styled text from a Model to be displayed on a View!

Displaying Rich Text Content in Your Views

To display the rich text content in your views, you can simply access the content attribute of your model. Rails automatically handles the rendering of the rich text content, including any embedded attachments.

```
<h1><%= @article.title %></h1>
<%= @article.content %>
```

Rails will take care of rendering the Trix content for you, meaning it takes the content and displays it as pure HTML. Now with this functionality and the code, you can edit it right away!

Advanced Action Text: Going Beyond the Basics

- **Customizing the Trix Editor:** You can customize the Trix editor by adding your own CSS styles and JavaScript code.
- **Using Custom Attachments:** You can create custom attachment types to handle specific types of content, such as videos or maps.
- **Storing Attachments:** Although it uses ActiveStorage by default, it can be pointed towards a different storage as well!

My "Rich Text Realization" Story: I used to dread dealing with rich text editing in web applications. It always seemed like a complex and time-consuming task. But once I discovered Action Text, it transformed the way I approached rich text editing. Action Text made it incredibly easy to add rich text editing to my applications, and it handled all the nitty-gritty details for me.

Key Takeaways:

- Action Text simplifies the process of creating and managing rich text content in Rails.
- Use the has_rich_text macro to add rich text content to your models.
- Use the rich_text_area helper to display the rich text editor in your forms.
- Customize the Trix editor and add custom attachment types to tailor Action Text to your specific needs.

By mastering Action Text, you'll be able to add rich and engaging content to your Rails applications with ease. This will significantly enhance the user experience and allow you to build more sophisticated and visually appealing applications.

13.2 Turbo 8 Integration: Rails Gets a Shot of Speed

You've mastered the fundamentals of Rails development. Now, it's time to supercharge your application's performance with **Turbo**. This is a set of powerful code that drastically improves web page experiences, most of which will be loaded and handled without you even knowing it!

Think of Turbo as a performance-enhancing elixir for your Rails application. It allows you to build fast and responsive user interfaces without the complexity of traditional JavaScript frameworks. You will need to know what these improvements do on the back end to have a full understanding on why Turbo is so powerful.

What is Turbo?

Turbo is a set of complementary techniques for building modern web applications:

- Turbo Drive
- Turbo Frames
- Turbo Streams

By combining these techniques, you can build web applications that feel like single-page applications (SPAs) without the complexity of managing a large JavaScript codebase. In addition, it also follows more HTML coding style over a JS mindset.

Turbo and Hotwire

Turbo is actually a part of the Hotwire system, which is used to build web applications. Turbo does not need to be used alone, as it was designed to work with all other concepts to create a good page.

Why Use Turbo?

- **Faster Page Loads:** Turbo Drive intelligently caches pages and prefetches links, resulting in faster page loads and a smoother user experience.
- **Partial Page Updates:** Turbo Frames allow you to update specific regions of the page without reloading the entire page, reducing bandwidth usage and improving responsiveness.
- **Real-Time Updates:** Turbo Streams enable you to push real-time updates to the client, creating a more engaging and interactive user experience.
- **Reduced JavaScript:** Turbo allows you to build complex web applications with minimal JavaScript.

1. Turbo Drive: Intelligent Page Navigation

Turbo Drive intercepts all link clicks and form submissions, and handles them using JavaScript, instead of relying on the browser to do a full page reload.

Key features of Turbo Drive:

- **Page Caching:** Turbo Drive caches pages in memory, allowing you to quickly navigate back and forth between pages without reloading them.
- **Form Submission Handling:** Turbo Drive handles form submissions using AJAX, updating the page without a full reload.
- **Progress Indicator:** Turbo Drive displays a progress indicator while the page is loading, providing feedback to the user.

No installation or setup is required! As long as you have added the default javascript file to the layout, turbo drive will be automatically set for the application. With Turbo Drive doing all the heavy loading on the site, users can seamlessly browse your application.

2. Turbo Frames: Targeted Content Updates

Turbo Frames allow you to break up your pages into smaller, independent sections that can be updated individually. This is useful for creating dynamic and responsive user interfaces without reloading the entire page. Also instead of passing everything from your method down through the webpage, you are able to send it to a specific area of the page!

Key features of Turbo Frames:

- **Lazy Loading:** Turbo Frames can be loaded lazily, only when they are needed.
- **Targeted Updates:** When a Turbo Frame is updated, only the content within the frame is replaced, minimizing the amount of data that needs to be transferred over the network. This minimizes load time, as browsers don't need to reload elements that have already loaded.
- **Independent Navigation:** Turbo Frames can have their own navigation history, allowing users to navigate within a frame without affecting the rest of the page.

To create a Turbo Frame, you can use the <turbo-frame> tag:

```
    <turbo-frame id="article_<%= article.id %>"> #set the
parameters for the turbo
  <h2><%= article.title %></h2>
  <p><%= article.text %></p>
</turbo-frame>
```

The id attribute is used to identify the frame. When you submit a form or click a link within the frame, Turbo Drive will automatically update the content of the frame with the response from the server.

3. Turbo Streams: Real-Time Content Updates

Turbo Streams allow you to push real-time updates to the client, creating a more engaging and interactive user experience.

Key features of Turbo Streams:

- **Server-Sent Events (SSE):** Turbo Streams use Server-Sent Events (SSE) to push updates from the server to the client.
- **DOM Manipulation:** Turbo Streams provide a set of actions for manipulating the DOM, such as appending, prepending, replacing, and removing elements.
- **Minimal JavaScript:** Turbo Streams allow you to implement real-time updates with minimal JavaScript.

To use Turbo Streams, you need to broadcast updates from your server.

```
    # app/models/article.rb
class Article < ApplicationRecord
  after_create_commit { broadcast_prepend_to "articles" }
#When a commit is created, make it live right away
  after_update_commit { broadcast_replace_to "articles" }
  after_destroy_commit { broadcast_remove_to "articles" }
end
```

Now users can create new features as soon as they update the new action on your models!
Also make sure to update

- Turbo::Streams::ActionHelper
- Turbo::StreamsTagHelper

My "Turbo Boost" Story: I was amazed to see the speed improvements and reduced boilerplate as I used it more. I can't wait to see what new advances and speed it allows us to perform.

Key Takeaways:

- Turbo is a set of techniques for building modern web applications by sending HTML over the wire.
- Turbo Drive, Turbo Frames, and Turbo Streams are the three core components of Turbo.
- Turbo can significantly improve the performance and responsiveness of your Rails applications.

By mastering Turbo, you'll be able to build blazing-fast web applications that deliver a great user experience. It's a game-changer for Rails development!

13.3 Hotwire: The Return to Server-Side Simplicity

You've explored traditional Rails development and perhaps even dabbled with JavaScript frameworks for building dynamic user interfaces. Now, let's explore a different approach: **Hotwire**.

Think of Hotwire as a return to server-side simplicity. It allows you to build modern, interactive web applications by sending HTML over the wire, rather than relying on complex JavaScript frameworks like React, Angular, or Vue. It will also simplify your deployment process.

What is Hotwire?

Hotwire (HTML Over The Wire) is a set of techniques for building modern web applications by sending HTML over the wire, instead of complex JSON responses. Hotwire consists of 3 major technologies

1. Turbo
2. Stimulus
3. Strada

Instead of building complex applications with lots of Javascript to set up, with Hotwire, you will mainly work with HTML and see the updates live.

Key Benefits of Hotwire:

- **Reduced Complexity:** Hotwire allows you to build complex web applications using simple HTML and server-side code. You can significantly reduce the amount of JavaScript in your application.
- **Improved Performance:** Hotwire delivers fast and responsive user experiences.
- **Enhanced Security:** By reducing the amount of JavaScript in your application, you can also reduce the attack surface and improve security.
- **Accessibility:** Hotwire promotes accessibility by using standard HTML elements.
- **Maintainability:** Hotwire applications are easier to maintain and update than traditional JavaScript-heavy applications.

Turbo: Supercharging Rails with HTML Over the Wire

Turbo is a key component of Hotwire that provides a set of techniques for building fast and responsive web applications using HTML over the wire. (You can find more information on how Turbo is integrated into Hotwire on Section 13.2)

Stimulus: Adding Sprinkle of JavaScript for Enhanced Interactivity

While Hotwire aims to minimize the amount of JavaScript in your application, there are still situations where you need to add a sprinkle of JavaScript to enhance interactivity.

Stimulus is a lightweight JavaScript framework that is designed to work seamlessly with Hotwire. It allows you to add small amounts of JavaScript code to your HTML elements to handle user interactions, such as button clicks, form submissions, and data updates.

With the use of Hotwire, you can have dynamic results in a simpler manner, and that is what Stimulus brings as well.
Key concepts in Stimulus:

- Data controllers
- Actions
- Targets

Here is some code!

```
<div data-controller="article-comments">
```

```
  <button data-action="click->article-
comments#toggleComments">
    Show Comments
  </button>

  <div data-article-comments-target="comments">
    <!-- Comments will go here -->
  </div>
</div>
```

With the javascript to back it.

```
    import { Controller } from "@hotwired/stimulus"
// Connects to data-controller="article-comments"
export default class extends Controller {
  static targets = [ "comments" ]

  toggleComments() {
    this.commentsTarget.classList.toggle("hidden") //toggle
the comments to be hidden
  }
}
```

Each controller follows a specific format that will then be set based on the div on the HTML. Note that if you load a library from an external source, this code won't work! You will need a separate JavaScript bundler (discussed in previous sections) to import all of these libraries to work.

Strada: Bridging Web and Native Mobile Apps

Strada is the newest component of the Hotwire framework. It enables you to reuse most of the code from the web app and create native mobile applications.

My "Hotwire Conversion" Story: I used to be a huge fan of JavaScript frameworks for building complex user interfaces. But as I worked on more and more Hotwire projects, I realized how much simpler, faster, and more maintainable it was to use HTML over the wire. The lack of a backend framework meant a lot more Javascript knowledge is involved and code is difficult to debug. Using Hotwire, with its built-in features that are easy to read, code has never been easier!

Key Takeaways:

- Hotwire is a set of techniques for building modern web applications by sending HTML over the wire.
- Hotwire reduces the complexity of building dynamic user interfaces and improves performance.
- Turbo, Stimulus, and Strada are the core components of Hotwire.

By embracing Hotwire, you'll be able to build faster, more maintainable, and more accessible Rails applications that deliver a great user experience. You will also need to put more consideration into what information you need and learn the different nuances of every command, but in general it will be easier to build applications from this point and forth!

13.4 Code Organization: The Architect's Blueprint

You've mastered the core concepts of Rails development and are building increasingly complex applications. Now, it's time to focus on a critical, and often overlooked, aspect of software engineering: **code organization**. Code Organization is what separates amateur from professional.

Think of code organization as the architect's blueprint for your application. A well-organized codebase is easy to understand, navigate, maintain, and extend. A poorly organized codebase, on the other hand, can become a tangled mess that is difficult to work with and prone to errors.

Why is Code Organization Important?

- **Readability:** Well-organized code is easier to read and understand, making it easier for other developers (and yourself in the future) to work on the project.
- **Maintainability:** Well-organized code is easier to maintain and update. You can make changes to the code without having to worry about breaking other parts of the application.
- **Testability:** Well-organized code is easier to test. You can write unit tests that focus on individual components of your application, ensuring that they are working correctly.
- **Scalability:** Well-organized code is easier to scale. You can add new features and functionality without affecting the performance or stability of the existing code.
- **Collaboration:** Well-organized code makes it easier for multiple developers to work on the same project simultaneously.

It will also save a lot of debugging and development time as it will be simpler to create what you need.

General Best Practices for Code Organization

Before diving into Rails-specific techniques, let's review some general best practices for code organization:

- **Follow the Single Responsibility Principle (SRP):** Each class, method, or module should have a single, well-defined responsibility. Avoid creating classes or methods that do too much.
- **Keep it DRY (Don't Repeat Yourself):** Avoid duplicating code. If you find yourself writing the same code in multiple places, extract it into a reusable method or class.
- **Use Meaningful Names:** Give your classes, methods, variables, and files descriptive names that clearly indicate their purpose.
- **Write Comments:** Use comments to explain complex code or to document the purpose of a class or method. However, avoid over-commenting. Code should be self-explanatory whenever possible.
- **Use Consistent Formatting:** Follow a consistent formatting style throughout your codebase. This makes it easier to read and understand the code. Tools like RuboCop can help enforce consistent formatting.
- **Keep Methods Short:** Keep your methods short and focused. If a method is too long or complex, break it up into smaller, more manageable methods. It's better to have lots of code than methods that are too big to handle!
- **Reduce coupling:** Make sure that one component does not need to know too much about another object. Use proper patterns such as inversion of dependency

Rails-Specific Code Organization Techniques

Rails provides several conventions and tools that help you organize your code:

- **Fat Model, Skinny Controller:** Move as much business logic as possible into your models, keeping your controllers lean and focused on handling requests and coordinating between models and views. You want most code to be placed in the model and that the controller just handles the flow.

- **Use Service Objects:** Encapsulate complex business logic in service objects, which are plain Ruby objects that perform a specific task. Service objects can help you keep your models and controllers clean and focused. To implement, you need to create a folder under /app such as /app/services and create those ruby classes within this directory.
- **Extract View Logic to Helpers:** Move complex view logic to helper methods to keep your views clean and readable.

Helper files can be created within app/helpers

- **Use Concerns:** Concerns are modules that can be included in multiple models or controllers to share common functionality. This can help you avoid code duplication. Be cautious with concerns, as they can sometimes make it difficult to understand the dependencies between your classes.
- **Custom Validators:** Add custom validators when validations start to get complex or are similar among many properties or models.

Here's an example of using concerns:

```ruby
# app/models/concerns/loggable.rb
module Loggable
  extend ActiveSupport::Concern

  included do
    after_create :log_creation
  end

  def log_creation
    Rails.logger.info "#{self.class.name} created with id:
#{self.id}"
  end
end

# app/models/article.rb
class Article < ApplicationRecord
  include Loggable
  # ...
end

# app/models/user.rb
class User < ApplicationRecord
  include Loggable
  # ...
end
```

In this example, the Loggable concern provides a log_creation method that is called after an object is created. This concern can be included in multiple models to add logging functionality to all of them.

My "Code Cleanup" Awakening: I used to think that code organization wasn't that important. But then I inherited a large Rails application that was poorly organized, and it took me weeks to figure out how everything worked. That's when I realized the value of a well-organized codebase and made it a priority on every project I worked on.

Key Takeaways:

- Code organization is essential for building maintainable, scalable, and collaborative codebases.
- Follow general best practices for code organization, such as SRP, DRY, and using meaningful names.
- Use Rails-specific techniques, such as fat model, skinny controller, service objects, and concerns.
- The goal is to provide structure and stability to the ever changing code design.

By embracing these code organization principles, you'll be able to build Rails applications that are not only functional but also a pleasure to work with.

13.5 Security Best Practices: Building Fort Knox for Your Web App

You've learned how to build the features of your Rails applications, but are those features secure? If not, you will risk leaking data, or allow bad actors from breaking your program. Security should not be an afterthought. Instead, by instilling best practices it ensures that the program is secure and maintainable!

Think of these security best practices as building a Fort Knox for your web app. Each measure adds another layer of defense, making it increasingly difficult for attackers to breach your security perimeter.

Importance of Security

- Secure application are required so end-users do not need to fear their personal information getting leaked. A good framework and design leads to secure and long-term users.
- With the constant updates and attacks, developers should continuously update to protect.
- Following security best practices can help prevent costly data breaches, reputational damage, and legal liabilities.

Key Security Areas

- **Keep Your Gems Up to Date:** Regularly update your gems to patch security vulnerabilities. Use bundle audit to identify any known vulnerabilities in your dependencies.

Vulnerable gems should not be in a project. As updates happen frequently, regularly update the gem.

- **Use Strong Parameters:** Always use strong parameters to protect your application from mass assignment vulnerabilities. This helps prevent users from updating properties that they should not access. It also is an issue from the controller as well!
- **Sanitize User Input:** Sanitize all user input before displaying it in your views to prevent cross-site scripting (XSS) attacks. Sanitize helpers should always be used before allowing a rendering that you have not personally typed.
- **Use HTTPS:** Always use HTTPS to encrypt communication between the client and the server. This is a default on most platforms and should be the base requirement for any code. This will be key in ensuring and complying with regulatory laws and customer expectations.
- **Use a Content Security Policy (CSP):** Implement a CSP to control which resources the browser is allowed to load. CSP helps prevent XSS attacks by limiting the sources from which scripts, stylesheets, and other resources can be loaded. Setting it as default is important.
- **Password Storage:** Never store passwords as plain text! Use bcrypt and always have password restrictions for the password's length, etc. This goes a long way to prevent bad actors from finding the passwords!
- **Implement Rate Limiting:** Rate limiting for both creating data and log in is very important so that brute force cannot be done on your authentication. This will prevent common attacks that are done from bots.

- **Be Cautious with File Uploads:** Be sure to set all the proper requirements with files being uploaded. Check for file sizes and also what type of files there are to prevent unintended injections.
- **Session Management:** Set expirations on all sessions and always use HTTPS so that connections cannot be intercepted.
- **Testing for Injections:**
  - Use a tool that test each point and sees the validity, especially for those to the database
  - If that is not available make sure that the tests are setup to handle if there is anything weird that passes to the database.
  - Always use test methods for different edge cases to ensure the data is valid

Here are a few extra security measures that you may want to try on top of this:

- **Secure File Downloads**
- **Secure Direct Object References (Insecure DO)**
- **Broken Authentication**

My "Security Scare" Story: Once upon a time, I thought that security was an overblown concern. Then, I accidentally left a debugging endpoint active that let anyone see user PII such as emails. Ever since then, that experience has taught me to be more careful and understand security is the first priority as a lead on each project.

Key Takeaways:

- Security should be a top priority for every Rails developer.
- Keep your gems up to date, use strong parameters, sanitize user input, and always use HTTPS.
- Implement a Content Security Policy (CSP) to control which resources the browser is allowed to load.
- Protect your application from brute-force attacks by implementing rate limiting.
- Stay informed about the latest security threats and vulnerabilities.

By embracing these security best practices, you'll be able to build more secure and trustworthy Rails applications that protect your users and their data. This is an ongoing process that requires constant vigilance and a commitment to security.

Chapter 14: Launching Your Creation - Deploying a Rails Application

You've poured your heart and soul into building your Rails application. Now, it's time for the grand finale: deployment! Getting your application live and accessible to users is a rewarding experience that marks the culmination of all your hard work. But the road is often perilous and comes with its share of difficulties!

Think of deployment as launching your rocket into orbit. It requires careful preparation, precise execution, and ongoing monitoring to ensure that your application reaches its destination and stays there.

14.1 Preparing Your Rails App for Deployment: T-Minus to Launch!

You've built your Rails application, meticulously crafting features and squashing bugs. Now, the moment of truth is approaching: deployment! But before you hit the "launch" button, it's crucial to take some time to properly prepare your application. Proper preparation can make the steps required much easier and manageable.

Think of this stage as your pre-flight checklist. Each item on the list is designed to ensure that your application is optimized, secure, and ready to handle the demands of the production environment. Skipping steps here could lead to crashes, security vulnerabilities, or poor performance.

The Importance of Environment Variables: Secret Keys and Beyond

One of the most important steps is to configure your environment variables. Environment variables are settings that are defined outside of your application code and are used to configure various aspects of your application, such as:

- **Database Credentials:** Username, password, host, and database name.
- **API Keys:** Keys for accessing third-party APIs.

241

- **Secret Keys:** Used to encrypt session data, generate CSRF tokens, and perform other security-sensitive operations.

Why Environment Variables are Crucial:

- **Security:** Storing sensitive information in environment variables prevents it from being hardcoded into your application code, which could be accidentally exposed in your version control system.
- **Configuration:** Environment variables allow you to easily configure your application for different environments (development, test, production) without modifying the code.
- **Flexibility:** Environment variables make it easy to change configuration settings without having to redeploy your application.

Managing Environment Variables: The .env File (Development)

During development, you can use a .env file to store your environment variables. The .env file is a plain text file that contains a list of key-value pairs, one per line.

To use a .env file, you'll need to install the dotenv gem:

1. Add the dotenv gem to your Gemfile:

```
group :development, :test do
  gem 'dotenv-rails'
end
```

2. Run bundle install:

```
bundle install
```

3. Create a .env file in the root directory of your application:

```
DATABASE_USERNAME=myuser
DATABASE_PASSWORD=mypassword
SECRET_KEY_BASE=your_secret_key_base
```

4. Access the environment variables in your code using the ENV hash:

```
database_username = ENV['DATABASE_USERNAME']
```

```
database_password = ENV['DATABASE_PASSWORD']
secret_key_base = ENV['SECRET_KEY_BASE']
```

Important Security Note: Never commit your .env file to your version control system. Add it to your .gitignore file to prevent it from being accidentally committed. If it is not in that gitignore, then your details will be leaked to the public!

Configuring Production Credentials (The Platform-Specific Approach)

In production, you won't be able to rely on the .env file. Instead, you'll need to configure your environment variables using the deployment platform's tools. Each platform has its own way of setting environment variables:

- **Heroku:** Use the heroku config:set command:

```
    heroku config:set DATABASE_USERNAME=your_username
DATABASE_PASSWORD=your_password
SECRET_KEY_BASE=your_secret_key_base
```

- **DigitalOcean:** Set environment variables in your server's configuration file (e.g., .bashrc, .zshrc) or using a tool like systemd.
- **AWS:** Use the AWS Management Console or the AWS CLI to set environment variables for your EC2 instances or other services.

Consult your deployment platform's documentation for specific instructions on how to set environment variables. If you are not using a platform like Heroku then it will take more setup.

Running Database Migrations

Database migrations are Ruby files that define changes to your database schema. Before deploying your application, you need to run your database migrations to create the necessary tables and columns.

To run your database migrations in production, use the rails db:migrate command:

```
    rails db:migrate
```

You may need to run this command on your server after deploying the code.

Precompiling Assets: Optimizing for Performance

The Asset Pipeline is responsible for compiling, minifying, and fingerprinting your assets (CSS, JavaScript, images). Precompiling your assets before deploying your application can significantly improve its performance.

To precompile your assets for production, run the following command:

```
rails assets:precompile
```

This will create a directory called public/assets that contains all of your precompiled assets.

My "Deployment Near-Miss" Story: I once deployed a Rails application to production without setting the SECRET_KEY_BASE environment variable. The application crashed immediately, and it took me a while to figure out what was going on. I learned the hard way that it's crucial to configure all of your environment variables correctly before deploying your application.

Key Takeaways:

- Environment variables are used to configure your application for different environments.
- Use a .env file to manage environment variables during development.
- Configure environment variables using your deployment platform's tools in production.
- Run database migrations to create the necessary tables and columns.
- Precompile your assets to improve performance.

By following these steps, you'll be well-prepared to deploy your Rails application to production and ensure that it is properly configured and ready to handle real-world traffic.

14.2 Choosing a Deployment Platform: Finding the Perfect Home for Your App

You've prepared your application for deployment. Now, the next big question is: where will it live? Choosing the right deployment platform is a critical decision that can impact your application's performance, scalability, cost, and maintainability.

Think of your deployment platform as the real estate on which your application will reside. You want to choose a location that is affordable, accessible, and provides the right amenities to support your application's needs.

Understanding Your Options: A Comparative Overview

There are many different platforms you can use to deploy your Rails application. Here's a look at some of the most popular options, categorized by their level of abstraction and control:

1. Platform-as-a-Service (PaaS): The Easy Button (Mostly)

PaaS providers offer a high level of abstraction, handling much of the underlying infrastructure and server management for you. This makes them easy to use, but they also offer less control over the environment.

- **Heroku:**
    - **Pros:** Extremely easy to use, free tier available for small projects, excellent documentation, large community.
    - **Cons:** Can be expensive for larger applications, limited control over the server environment.
    - **Good For:** Beginners, small to medium-sized projects, applications that require rapid deployment and scalability.

2. Infrastructure-as-a-Service (IaaS): More Control, More Responsibility

IaaS providers offer more control over the server environment, but they also require you to handle more of the underlying infrastructure management.

- **DigitalOcean:**

- o **Pros:** Affordable pricing, simple and intuitive interface, good documentation.
- o **Cons:** Requires more configuration and management than PaaS providers.
- o **Good For:** Developers who want more control over their server environment and are comfortable with basic system administration tasks.
- **Amazon Web Services (AWS):**
  - o **Pros:** Comprehensive set of services, highly scalable and reliable, pay-as-you-go pricing.
  - o **Cons:** Can be complex and overwhelming, requires significant expertise to manage.
  - o **Good For:** Complex applications that require high scalability, reliability, and a wide range of services.
- **Google Cloud Platform (GCP):**
  - o **Pros:** Similar to AWS, GCP offers a wide range of services for deploying and managing applications.
  - o **Cons:** Similar to AWS, GCP can be complex and overwhelming.
  - o **Good For:** Similar to AWS, GCP is well-suited for complex applications that require high scalability and reliability.

3. Containerization (With Docker): Maximum Flexibility

Containerization involves packaging your application and its dependencies into a self-contained unit called a container. This container can then be deployed to any environment that supports Docker, providing maximum flexibility and portability.

This can be hosted by yourself or through a service that sets it up.

- **Self Hosted**
  - o **Pros:** High level of control
  - o **Cons:** You must figure out how to serve your image
- **AWS Elastic Container Service (ECS):**
  - o **Pros:** AWS handles all the back end to set up the docker
  - o **Cons:** If you are not well versed in AWS it may be more difficult to deploy

Choosing a Deployment Platform: Key Factors to Consider

When choosing a deployment platform, consider the following factors:

- **Cost:** How much will it cost to run your application on the platform? Consider the cost of servers, databases, storage, bandwidth, and other services.
- **Scalability:** Can the platform handle your application's traffic and data volume as it grows? Can you easily scale your application up or down as needed?
- **Control:** How much control do you have over the server environment? Do you need to be able to customize the operating system, install specific software, or configure the network?
- **Ease of Use:** How easy is it to deploy and manage your application on the platform? Does the platform provide a user-friendly interface and good documentation?
- **Security:** Does the platform provide adequate security measures to protect your application and data?
- **Integration with other services:** If you use a lot of a certain product, you may want to choose a deployment platform that's designed around this framework.

For beginners Heroku is the easiest to use. Heroku makes it easier for beginners to handle all of the heavy lifting, and you can learn and build with that framework.

Recommendations for Beginners

If you're new to Rails development and deployment, I recommend starting with **Heroku**. Its ease of use and free tier make it an excellent choice for learning the basics of deployment and getting your application live quickly.

Once you become more comfortable with deployment, you can explore other platforms that offer more control and scalability, such as DigitalOcean or AWS. However, be prepared for a steeper learning curve.

My "Deployment Platform Hopping" Story: I've deployed Rails applications to a variety of different platforms over the years, and I've learned that there's no one-size-fits-all solution. Each platform has its own strengths and weaknesses, and the best choice depends on the specific needs of your application.

Key Takeaways:

- There are many different platforms you can use to deploy your Rails application.

247

- Consider cost, scalability, control, ease of use, and security when choosing a deployment platform.
- Heroku is a good choice for beginners.
- DigitalOcean and AWS offer more control and scalability but require more expertise.

By carefully considering your options and choosing the right deployment platform, you'll be well-prepared to share your Rails applications with the world.

14.3 Configuring Your Server and Database: Hardening the Foundation

You've chosen your deployment platform. Now, it's time to dive deeper and configure the underlying infrastructure that will power your Rails application. This involves setting up your server, configuring your database, and ensuring that all the pieces are working together seamlessly.

Think of this as building a solid foundation for your application. A well-configured server and database are essential for ensuring that your application runs smoothly, efficiently, and securely. These are what will cause issues and be what you spend time working on.

What You'll Need:

This chapter assumes you have a deployment platform in mind. Each platform will have its own tools and requirements, but most of them will cover most of the concepts that we will cover.

Server Configuration (for IaaS and Self-Managed Platforms)

If you're using a Platform-as-a-Service (PaaS) provider like Heroku, much of this configuration will be handled automatically. However, if you're using an Infrastructure-as-a-Service (IaaS) provider like DigitalOcean or AWS, or if you're managing your own server, you'll need to configure the server yourself.

Here are some of the key steps:

1. **Choose a Web Server:** Select a web server to handle incoming HTTP requests and serve your Rails application. Two popular options are Nginx and Apache. Nginx is generally preferred for its performance and scalability.
2. **Install a Web Server:** Install your chosen web server on your server. The specific steps will vary depending on your operating system and distribution.
3. **Configure a Virtual Host:** Create a virtual host configuration for your Rails application. This tells the web server how to handle requests for your domain name.

Here is some code for a simple webserver setup.

```
    server {
  listen 80;
  server_name example.com; #This is where your domain name
is.
  root /var/www/myapp/public;

  passenger_enabled on; #This enables the passenger to run
your ruby app
  rails_env production; #This is the environment that is used
}
```

Key elements of webserver config:

- listen 80: This configures a listener on Port 80, the standard port for all web pages.
- server_name example.com: This is the name for your server, be sure to actually link it to your domain.
- root /var/www/myapp/public: This is where your HTML files will reside. If it does not exist, your request will not load.
- passenger_enabled on: This tag turns the server settings on.

1. **Configure a Reverse Proxy:** Configure the web server to act as a reverse proxy, forwarding requests to your application server (e.g., Puma, Unicorn). This helps improve performance and security.

If the passenger does not load, then also consider having something like gunicorn, as a last resort.

Database Configuration: Connecting to Your Data

Your Rails application needs to be able to connect to your production database. This involves configuring the config/database.yml file with the correct database settings.

1. **Set Environment Variables:** As you learned in the previous section, never store your database credentials directly in the database.yml file. Instead, use environment variables to store sensitive information:

```
    production:
  adapter: postgresql
  encoding: unicode
  database: myapp_production
  pool: 5
  username: <%= ENV["DATABASE_USERNAME"] %> #Connects to the
username, password, and port to access
  password: <%= ENV["DATABASE_PASSWORD"] %>
  host: <%= ENV["DATABASE_HOST"] %>
  port: <%= ENV["DATABASE_PORT"] %>
```

A Word of Caution: Be sure that all the necessary objects actually exist on the system, and that the service is running. If that is not set up the entire page will not load and crash.

My "Infrastructure Nightmare" Story: I once spent days troubleshooting a deployment issue only to discover that the problem was a simple misconfiguration in the database connection settings. I had accidentally typed the wrong password in the database.yml file, and it was causing the application to crash. I learned the hard way that even the smallest configuration error can have a big impact on your application's stability.

Key Takeaways:

- Configuring your server and database is essential for a successful deployment.
- Choose a web server and configure it to serve your Rails application.
- Configure your database connection settings in the config/database.yml file.
- Use environment variables to store sensitive information.
- Pay close attention to detail and test your configuration thoroughly.

By taking the time to properly configure your server and database, you'll be able to create a solid foundation for your Rails application that can handle the demands of the production environment.

14.4 Deployment Steps and Troubleshooting: From Localhost to Live!

You've prepped your application and configured your server and database. Now, it's time for the moment you've been waiting for: deploying your application to the world!

Think of this as the launch sequence for your web application. Each step is critical, and a misstep at any point can lead to a failed launch.

It should also be a skill you are constantly improving on and developing so it will become much easier for you in the future.

Choosing a Deployment Strategy

There are two main deployment strategies for Rails applications:

- **Direct Deployment:** Deploy your application directly to a server using tools like Git, Capistrano, or SSH.
- **Containerized Deployment:** Package your application and its dependencies into a Docker container and deploy the container to a container orchestration platform like Kubernetes or AWS ECS.

We will use Git for this code!

Direct Deployment with Git Checklist*

Before the final deployment here are some things to consider

1. **Checklist all of the required gems installed on the service!** This will most likely lead to code crashing if you do not do this.
2. **Setting the Server Environment:** Many servers have unique system settings or configurations that is different from your computer!
3. **Testing the set up correctly!** The test section also applies to testing new versions, be sure to test it thoroughly to avoid regressions.
4. **Back up the data!** Ensure that you save a copy so that you have the ability to re-apply everything in the event of a deployment or error.

With that said the steps for using Git:

1. **Git Initialize the Code**: After getting the code up to date, initialize a git repo on the code.

```
git init
```

This allows Git to start tracking from the current point forward to have the code changes tracked. You may or may not have all of your .env or credential files on this file!

```
touch .gitignore
```

This creates a file to track which ones won't be committed to the git! After doing this, also set the branch of your local Git repo.

```
git branch -M main
```

Set the code to be main.

Then on a place such as GitHub, create a new code repository for the project.

1. Push to Github

Set up the git path to the source

```
git remote add origin <link to code>
```

Create a standard commit pattern

```
git commit -m "initial commit to set up the deployment"
git push origin main
```

Now at this point your codebase is all set, you need to pull the trigger for deployment for the code!

General Steps for any Deployment

1. Setting the env file in the right spot, along with necessary permissions to have the backend access it

252

2. Ensure that the postgresql is setup properly, and with the right settings. You can use RAILS_ENV=production rails db:setup to set it up.
3. Make sure to run bundle install
4. Make sure to run RAILS_ENV=production rails assets:precompile
5. Then start your engine with bundle exec rails s -e production

Check the output and make sure no errors popped up! Now your new service should be live!

Key Takeaways from the example code

- This works well if you have a test environment and the file is on Git. For manual and fresh installs will be very difficult. As such this is for the most simple way to do things, but has the least tools.

Troubleshooting Common Deployment Issues

Deployments never go perfectly. Here are some common issues, be sure to test frequently to catch problems that arise.

- **Database Connection Errors:**
  o **Problem:** Your application can't connect to the database.
  o **Solution:** Double-check your database credentials in config/database.yml and ensure that the database server is running and accessible. Verify the database settings with heroku config:get DATABASE_URL
- **Asset Compilation Errors:**
  o **Problem:** Your assets (CSS, JavaScript, images) are not being served correctly.
  o **Solution:** Make sure you have precompiled your assets correctly. Sometimes you have to re-run these commands. Also ensure that the asset paths in your views are correct, and try using RAILS_ENV=production rails assets:clobber and run precompile again
- **Missing Dependencies:**
  o **Problem:** Your application is missing required gems.
  o **Solution:** Run bundle install in the production environment to install all the necessary gems.
- **Server Configuration Errors:**
  o **Problem:** Your web server is not configured correctly.

- **Solution:** Review your web server configuration to ensure that it is correctly serving your Rails application. Review access and ensure the right people are able to see the web server.
- **Permission Issues:**
  - **Problem:** Your application doesn't have the necessary permissions to access certain files or directories.
  - **Solution:** Check file permissions to ensure that the web server has access to the application files.

My "Deployment Disaster Turned Triumph" Story: I will never forget my first major deployment. A lot of code worked, but the database table name was incorrect and caused the entire system to crash. The database was not connected right and nothing worked. Take your time, double check all of the work, and you'll find the answers!

Key Takeaways:

- Choose a deployment strategy that meets your needs.
- Follow a systematic approach to deploying your application.
- Be prepared to troubleshoot common deployment issues.
- Test your application thoroughly after deployment.

By following these steps, you'll be well-prepared to navigate the launch sequence and successfully deploy your Rails applications to production. Congratulations on reaching this milestone!

14.5 Post-Deployment Maintenance: Nurturing Your Live Application

You've successfully deployed your Rails application. Pat yourself on the back! However, deployment is not the finish line; it's just the starting point. Now, the real work begins: ensuring that your application remains healthy, stable, and secure over time.

Think of post-deployment maintenance as tending to a garden. You need to regularly water, weed, and fertilize your plants to ensure that they thrive. Similarly, you need to monitor your application, address any issues that arise, and keep it up-to-date to ensure that it continues to provide a great user experience.

The Importance of Post-Deployment Maintenance

- **Reliability:** Regular maintenance helps ensure that your application remains stable and available to your users.
- **Performance:** Ongoing monitoring and optimization can help improve your application's performance.
- **Security:** Staying up-to-date with security patches and best practices helps protect your application from vulnerabilities.
- **User Satisfaction:** A well-maintained application provides a better user experience, leading to increased user satisfaction.
- **Long-Term Cost Savings:** Proactive maintenance can help prevent costly problems down the road.

1. Continuous Monitoring: Keeping a Constant Watch

Monitoring your application is essential for identifying and addressing issues before they impact your users. There are several tools you can use for monitoring:

- **Server Logs:** Review your server logs regularly to identify any errors or potential problems.
- **Exception Tracking Services (e.g., Sentry, Airbrake):** Use an exception tracking service to automatically capture and report any exceptions that occur in your application. It's like a bug vacuum, sucking up all the errors and notifying you.

If anything has gone wrong, and the program is still accessible to the world, you should be able to have a monitor for it!

2. Regular Backups: Protecting Your Data

Backups are essential for protecting against data loss due to hardware failures, software errors, or security breaches.

- It is a good practice to have it setup and working before the application is deployed!
- **Database Backups:** Set up automated database backups to a secure location (e.g., Amazon S3, Google Cloud Storage).
- **Application Code Backups:** Back up your application code to a version control system (e.g., Git) and consider creating regular snapshots of your server environment.

- **Verify Backups:** Periodically test your backups to ensure that they are working correctly and that you can restore your data if necessary.

3. Security Audits: Staying One Step Ahead

Perform regular security audits to identify and fix any vulnerabilities in your application.

- **Static Analysis Tools:** Use static analysis tools to scan your codebase for potential security vulnerabilities.
- **Penetration Testing:** Hire a security expert to perform penetration testing to simulate real-world attacks and identify vulnerabilities.

4. Dependency Updates and Maintenance

The best way to make your application more secure and well performing is to stay current with the dependency updates,

- **Review Dependency Updates:** Stay informed about new releases of Rails and your gems.
- **Test Thoroughly:** Before deploying any dependency updates, test your application thoroughly to ensure that everything is working correctly. This helps to ensure that there are no regressions or new bugs.

5. Database Optimization: Scaling the Application

As your application grows, you may need to optimize your database to improve performance. This can involve:

- **Indexing:** Add indexes to frequently queried columns to speed up database queries.
- **Query Optimization:** Analyze and optimize slow-running SQL queries.
- **Caching:** Implement caching to reduce the load on your database.

In addition to these tips, you also want to watch the following:

- Database size increasing at large amounts
- Requests taking longer amounts of time
- Requests exceeding the limits.

All of these are signals for possible database updates.

My "Maintenance Misstep" Story: When everything was working at 100%, nothing bad can happen, right? So I pushed new code to production which ended up corrupting database data and crashing the website for hours. Set up alerts or use exception catching systems so that you know if a production is broken or errors exist! Also, set up backup data so that you do not corrupt any essential files from the database!

Key Takeaways:

- Post-deployment maintenance is essential for ensuring that your application remains healthy, stable, and secure.
- Monitor your application regularly, perform regular backups, and apply security updates.
- Optimize your database to improve performance as your application grows.
- Always consider users: are they able to access content? Can they contact you?

By embracing these post-deployment maintenance practices, you'll be able to build Rails applications that stand the test of time and provide a great user experience for years to come.

Chapter 15: Next Steps: Embarking on Your Rails Odyssey

Congratulations! You've reached the end of this introductory guide to Rails development. You've learned the fundamentals, built your first applications, and explored best practices for building robust and maintainable code. But what now? The web development landscape is wide and ever changing.

Think of this chapter as your compass and map for the next stage of your Rails adventure. It provides you with the resources, inspiration, and guidance you need to continue learning, growing, and contributing to the Rails community. You are never really done with Rails.

15.1 Building Your Rails Library: Knowledge is Your Greatest Asset

You've reached the end of this book, but this is not the end of the road. You need access to new content so that you are able to continue to learn!

Think of this section as building your personal Rails library, a collection of resources that you can draw upon throughout your web development journey. This is just a first step.

The Official Rails Documentation: The Source of Truth

First and foremost, familiarize yourself with the official Rails Documentation (https://guides.rubyonrails.org/). This is the single source of truth for all things Rails. It's well-organized, comprehensive, and always up-to-date. When you have a question about how Rails works, this should be your first stop. It will also provide the correct format and version to what you need, if needed.

- The API: This is where you find all specific methods, modules and properties with proper usages
- The guides: The guides walk you through different concepts of Rails and you are able to work with it very effectively!

Rails Guides: In-Depth Explanations and Practical Examples

The Rails Guides (https://guides.rubyonrails.org/) provide in-depth explanations of various Rails concepts and features, along with practical examples and code snippets. They're a great resource for learning more about specific topics or for getting a better understanding of how Rails works under the hood. The reason why these are useful is that the community maintains a lot of this and they take best practice into account to be sure that everything is accurate.

Some of the most useful guides include:

- **Getting Started with Rails:** A step-by-step guide to building your first Rails application.
- **Active Record Basics:** An introduction to Active Record, the ORM that Rails uses to interact with databases.
- **Action Controller Overview:** A comprehensive guide to Rails controllers and routing.
- **Active Support Core Extensions:** A guide to the many useful extensions that Rails adds to the Ruby standard library.
- **Testing Rails Applications:** A guide to using Minispec to test your Rails application
- **Security:** A guide to securing your application and what to expect from best practices.

Books for Deepening Your Knowledge

While online resources are great, sometimes you need a more structured and in-depth explanation of a topic. Here are a few recommended books for deepening your Rails knowledge:

- **"Agile Web Development with Rails 7":** This book goes deep into the subject with a good foundation with Rails. They are updated regularly, and can serve as your go to source in different use cases.
- **"The Rails 6 Way":** Although targeted at Rails 6, this book dives deep into Rails conventions, patterns, and best practices, providing a solid foundation for building scalable and maintainable applications. The lessons are applicable to later versions of rails, but you should be sure to check against the official documentation for any API changes. It also covers key concepts not specific to just Rails such as Inversion of Dependency which, while you might not use these things in practice, knowing about them will make you a better developer.

Online Communities: Connecting with Fellow Rails Developers

The Rails community is one of the most active and supportive communities in the web development world. There are many online communities where you can connect with other Rails developers, ask questions, and share your knowledge. These people often know a lot, and this is a great community to connect.

Some popular online communities include:

- **The Official Rails Forum:** A great place to ask questions, get help with problems, and discuss Rails-related topics.
- **Stack Overflow:** A Q&A site where you can find answers to almost any Rails-related question.
- **Reddit (r/rails):** A community where you can share links, ask questions, and discuss Rails-related news and articles.
- **Discord Communities** There are discord communities for specific gems or for new web development where you are able to ask, learn, and help out.

The Rails community are very helpful and you should always be open to connecting!

The Ruby Toolbox: Gems Galore!

The Ruby Toolbox (https://www.ruby-toolbox.com/) is a comprehensive directory of Ruby gems and resources. You can use Ruby Toolbox to find gems that can help you solve specific problems in your applications. Make sure to also consider the gem's maintainability and long-term use before committing.

My "Resource Roundup" Story: There's nothing more satisfying for me than when I can quickly find the answer that I need. If you are unable to immediately find the answer, you must persevere and find what is needed to finish the code! The key thing to know is the source and how useful that can be.

Key Takeaways:

- The official Rails Documentation is the single source of truth for all things Rails.
- Rails Guides provide in-depth explanations and practical examples.
- Books can provide a more structured and comprehensive understanding of Rails concepts.

- Online communities offer a great way to connect with other Rails developers and get help with problems.
- The Ruby Toolbox is a comprehensive directory of Ruby gems and resources.

By building your Rails library, you'll be well-prepared to tackle any challenge that comes your way and continue growing as a Rails developer. As you go, learn the different aspects of each so that you can more quickly and efficiently solve new problems!

15.2 Level Up: Advanced Rails Topics for the Aspiring Master

You've grasped the core concepts of Rails, built your first applications, and mastered the fundamentals of testing and deployment. Now it's time to explore the advanced topics that will elevate your skills and enable you to build truly sophisticated and scalable web applications. You are just getting started and these techniques will help you create a next gen application.

Think of these advanced topics as unlocking new abilities. As a player upgrades their character to be better, these are some of the options that you will have as a programmer.

APIs: Building Backends for a Connected World

- **What they are:** RESTful APIs are a critical building block for modern web applications. An API (Application Programming Interface) allows different applications to communicate with each other over the internet. An API will help with various functions such as
    - Allow data sharing for the web applications
    - Integrate with native Mobile Apps
    - Be made available for partner vendors
- **Key Concepts:** REST, JSON, authentication, authorization, versioning. It also lets you use the REST to allow different services.

Authorization: fine-Grained Permissions to Lock it Down

- **What it is:** While this book has talked about authentications using Devise, a much more complex method may be required. Learn how to implement fine-grained authorization schemes that provide granular control over user access to resources. This will help with creating more complex business rules for the different roles that the users play!

The gems that can be used are:

- CanCanCan
- Pundit
- Access Control List (ACL) to handle the business logic

Action Cable: Create a Realtime Web

- **What It Is:** The Action Cable allows the use of Ruby to display real-time web features. An API is often used and then called by the server to get things loaded. This is key for a real time website.

Key concepts:

- Redis for connection to the server.
- Implementation and connection to front end.

Queuing Backend

- **What It Is:** Asynchronous events happen all the time on the internet. Email being sent, text messages, images being processed are just a few. Implementing a queue helps you to move the processing to the background and allow users to not need to wait for the various requests, while the program is still being processed.
- **How to Implement:** DelayedJob gem is one to add this functionality

Testing

- **Why It Is:** While the scope of this book doesn't cover how to unit test, integration, or system test, understanding how to write code, the most important thing is to have the functionality running and protected.
- **Tips:** Be sure to use great names, focus on what the function needs to do, and that edge cases are well handled

Database Tuning, Optimization, and Sharding

- **Why It Is:** As your data volume grows, you may need to optimize your database to improve performance. This can involve techniques such as:

  *Indexing to increase performance to query.
  *Caching data from the database instead of calling each time.
  *Sharding data to different parts of the database

It also allows for scaling different services appropriately when everything is working efficiently.

How I Overcame Difficulty: The key part is to understand where each component fits within a codebase and their relationships with each other. You can then take advantage of all these services to create a well oiled machine!

Key Takeaways:

- Take the next challenge to learn more about the functions listed!
- Continue to learn from resources about advanced methods.
- With a little time, you will understand more advanced Rails concepts!

By exploring these advanced topics, you'll be able to build more sophisticated and scalable Rails applications that meet the needs of demanding users and complex business requirements. This is how you are able to grow from novice to advanced in coding.

15.3 Building Your Portfolio: Showcasing Your Awesome Creations

You've learned the skills and built some projects. Now it is time to show those off and get noticed! You need to build out a portfolio that will showcase to employers what you can offer them. This portfolio, the place you tell about your work and skills, will be your guide in the professional world.

Think of your portfolio as your digital resume, a collection of your best work that demonstrates your skills and abilities to potential employers or clients. A great portfolio should not just show what you've done, but also *why* you made certain decisions and what you learned along the way.

Why is a Portfolio Important?

- **Showcase Your Skills:** A portfolio is the best way to showcase your skills and abilities to potential employers or clients.
- **Demonstrate Your Experience:** A portfolio demonstrates your experience and shows that you have a proven track record of building successful Rails applications.
- **Stand Out from the Crowd:** A well-designed portfolio can help you stand out from the crowd of other job applicants or freelancers.
- **Prove Your Value:** A portfolio provides evidence that you can deliver value to potential employers or clients.
- **Help Others:** By showing others your past, they can see what kind of help or inspiration you bring, and it will get people coming.

Key Elements of a Strong Rails Portfolio

1. **A Variety of Projects:** Your portfolio should include a variety of projects that demonstrate your skills in different areas of Rails development. Include web apps and also APIs.
2. **Source Code on GitHub:** Make the source code for your projects publicly available on GitHub. This allows potential employers or clients to review your code and assess your coding style and skills. Also, remember to have a README.md page so that others can have an understanding of what is going on.
3. **Clean and Well-Documented Code:** Your code should be clean, well-organized, and easy to understand. Use meaningful names for your classes, methods, and variables, and add comments to explain complex code or to document the purpose of a class or method.
4. **Clear Descriptions of Projects:** For each project in your portfolio, write a clear and concise description that explains:
   - The purpose of the project.
   - The technologies used.
   - The key features.
   - The challenges you faced and how you overcame them.
   - What you learned from the project.
5. **Live Demos (if possible):** If possible, provide live demos of your projects so that potential employers or clients can try them out for themselves. You can use platforms like Heroku, DigitalOcean, or AWS to host your demos.
6. **A Personal Touch:** Add a personal touch to your portfolio to showcase your personality and passion for web development. Include

a brief biography, a photo, and a statement of your goals and aspirations.

If you want to get more attention, try to create something that you think would be used and have others test it out.

Project Ideas to Get You Started

Here are a few project ideas that you can use to build your Rails portfolio:

- **Blog Engine:**
- **Task Management Application:**
- **E-commerce Store:**
- **Social Networking Site:**

Make sure that any of these has a unique addition to it so that you show that you have added a feature.

Make it User Friendly: Put yourself into the mind of a user. By putting it through their perspective you can greatly expand on what you are building!

Don't Be Afraid to Show Your Imperfect Code

While it's important to strive for excellence, don't be afraid to include projects in your portfolio that are not perfect. Showing your ability to learn, adapt, and overcome challenges is just as important as showcasing your successes. Just be sure that you are working on the right things so the portfolio does not become useless.

In such case you should:

- Add what you tried to do
- What you tried
- What steps to take next for yourself or for anyone else.

My "Portfolio Pivot" Story: I spent way too much time trying to make each piece of my portfolio to perfection. But in doing so, nothing actually reached to the world! Now it is better to release smaller less tested code that people can contribute to and use than having one amazing application that nobody knows.

Key Takeaways:

- A portfolio is essential for showcasing your Rails skills and attracting potential employers or clients.
- Include a variety of projects, source code on GitHub, clear descriptions, and live demos (if possible).
- Don't be afraid to show your imperfect code and share what you learned from your experiences.
- Be open to feedback and remember to always be innovating!

By building a strong portfolio, you'll be able to demonstrate your skills, showcase your experience, and stand out from the crowd in the competitive world of web development. This is what you can do with everything you have done so far! Good luck!

15.4 Contributing to Open Source: Leaving Your Mark on the Digital World

You've learned how to build Rails applications. Now, it's time to take your skills to the next level by contributing to open source projects. In addition, you can continue learning and discover ways to express yourself!

Think of contributing to open source as leaving your mark on the digital world. You're not just building applications for yourself, you're helping to build the tools and libraries that thousands of other developers use every day. It's a chance to learn, collaborate, and make a real difference.

Why Contribute to Open Source?

- **Improve Your Skills:** Contributing to open source is a great way to improve your coding skills. You'll have the opportunity to work with experienced developers, learn new techniques, and get feedback on your code.
- **Learn from Others:** Open-source projects are collaborative efforts. By working with other developers, you'll learn from their experiences and gain new perspectives.
- **Build Your Network:** Contributing to open source is a great way to build your network and connect with other developers in the Rails community.
- **Give Back to the Community:** Contributing to open source is a way to give back to the community and help make Rails a better framework for everyone.
- Show and Provide a good product for your future career

- Make friends and contacts with developers you will work with.

Where to Find Open Source Projects to Contribute To

Here are some places to find open-source projects to contribute to:

- **GitHub:** GitHub is the home of most open-source Rails projects. You can search for projects based on language, topic, and other criteria.
- **Ruby Toolbox:** The Ruby Toolbox lists many popular gems, including information on how to contribute to each project.
- Look at what gems are currently being used.
- See if they meet the needs that you need them to.
- If not, you can implement and then request them to be a part of the main build!

Ways to Contribute to Open Source (Even as a Beginner)

Contributing to open source doesn't have to be intimidating. There are many ways to contribute, even if you're a beginner:

- **Fix Bugs:** Find and fix bugs in existing projects. This is a great way to get started, as it doesn't require a lot of experience.
- **Add Features:** Add new features to existing projects. This is a more challenging way to contribute, but it can be very rewarding.
- **Write Documentation:** Improve the documentation for existing projects. This is a great way to contribute if you enjoy writing and have a knack for explaining things clearly.
- **Create Tutorials:** Create tutorials to help other developers learn how to use Rails. This is a great way to share your knowledge and help others get started with Rails.
- **Review Code:** Review code submitted by other contributors. This helps ensure that the code is high-quality and follows the project's coding standards.
- **Triage Issues:** Help triage issues by confirming bugs, providing additional information, and assigning labels.
- **Improve Accessibility:** Helping users with disabilities connect and use the software can also be a great goal.
- **Translations:** Help to translate your code to different languages.

Steps to Contribute to Open Source

Here's a general outline of the steps involved in contributing to an open-source project:

1. **Find a Project:** Find an open-source project that you're interested in contributing to.
2. **Review the Project's Guidelines:** Review the project's contributing guidelines to understand the project's coding standards, workflow, and communication channels.
3. **Find an Issue:** Find an issue that you want to work on. If there are no existing issues that interest you, you can create a new issue.
4. **Fork the Repository:** Fork the project's repository on GitHub.
5. **Create a Branch:** Create a new branch in your forked repository to work on your changes. Give the branch a descriptive name that reflects the purpose of your changes (e.g., fix-bug-123, add-new-feature).
6. **Make Your Changes:** Make your changes to the code. Follow the project's coding standards and best practices.
7. **Test Your Changes:** Write tests to ensure that your changes are working correctly and that they don't introduce any new bugs.
8. **Commit Your Changes:** Commit your changes with clear and descriptive commit messages.
9. **Push Your Branch:** Push your branch to your forked repository on GitHub.
10. **Create a Pull Request:** Create a pull request to submit your changes to the original repository.
11. **Respond to Feedback:** Respond to any feedback that you receive from the project maintainers.
12. **Iterate:** Incorporate feedback into your code and resubmit until approval.

My "Open Source Epiphany" Story:

Contributing to open source is a chance to contribute to the greater community. In the future, I think every developer should contribute to open source so that we can make the world a better place!

Key Takeaways:

- Contributing to open source is a great way to improve your skills, learn from experienced developers, and give back to the community.
- You can contribute to open source in many ways, even if you're a beginner.

- Look for open-source projects on platforms like GitHub.

By contributing to open source, you'll not only improve your skills and build your network but also make a real difference in the world of software development.

15.5 Glimpsing the Horizon: The Future of Rails and Web Development

You've reached the end of our journey through the fundamentals of Rails. But technology constantly evolves, and the most successful developers are those who never stop learning and exploring. Here's what to expect!

Think of this chapter as gazing into a crystal ball, trying to discern the trends and technologies that will shape the future of Rails and web development. By staying ahead of the curve, you'll be well-prepared to adapt to new challenges and opportunities.

Rails: Evolving with the Times

Rails itself is constantly evolving. The core team and community are dedicated to keeping Rails relevant and competitive in the ever-changing web development landscape. Some areas to watch for advancements:

- **Hotwire and Turbo:** The focus on server-rendered HTML with enhanced interactivity is likely to continue. Expect further improvements to Turbo and Stimulus, as well as new tools and techniques for building Hotwire applications.
- **API-First Development:** While Rails has always been a great framework for building full-stack web applications, there's a growing trend towards building API-first applications that serve data to a variety of clients (e.g., web browsers, mobile apps, IoT devices).
- **Performance Optimization:** The Rails team is constantly working on performance optimizations, both at the framework level and in the underlying Ruby runtime.
- **Security:** Security is always a top priority for the Rails team. Expect continued improvements to the framework's security features and best practices.

Key Trends in Web Development: Broader Perspectives

Beyond Rails itself, there are several key trends in web development that you should be aware of:

- **JavaScript Frameworks (React, Angular, Vue):** While Hotwire aims to reduce the need for JavaScript, these frameworks are still widely used for building complex user interfaces. Understanding JavaScript frameworks can be valuable, especially if you need to integrate Rails with existing JavaScript-heavy applications.
- **Serverless Computing:** Serverless computing platforms like AWS Lambda and Google Cloud Functions allow you to run code without managing servers. This can significantly reduce the cost and complexity of deploying and managing web applications.
- **Progressive Web Apps (PWAs):** PWAs are web applications that provide a native app-like experience in the browser. PWAs offer features such as offline support, push notifications, and installability. These can be amazing for areas without reliable data, and can also be more simple to test and work with when they are available.
- **WebAssembly:** WebAssembly (Wasm) is a new technology that allows you to run high-performance code in the browser. This opens up new possibilities for web applications, such as running computationally intensive tasks or porting existing desktop applications to the web.
- **AI-Assisted Development:** Artificial intelligence (AI) is increasingly being used to assist developers with tasks such as code completion, bug detection, and code generation. Tools like GitHub Copilot can help you write code faster and with fewer errors.

Adapting to Change: Your Key to Success

The web development landscape is constantly evolving. The most important thing you can do to stay ahead of the curve is to embrace a growth mindset and be willing to learn new things.

Here are some tips for staying up-to-date:

- **Read Blogs and Articles:** Follow industry blogs and publications to stay informed about the latest trends and technologies.
- **Attend Conferences and Meetups:** Attend conferences and meetups to learn from experts and connect with other developers.
- **Take Online Courses:** Take online courses to learn new skills and technologies.

- **Experiment with New Tools:** Try out new tools and technologies to see how they can improve your workflow.
- **Contribute to Open Source:** Contributing to open-source projects is a great way to learn new things and stay up-to-date with the latest trends.

My "Future Vision" Story: If the past is anything to go by, it should come as no shock that new technologies replace old ones in a matter of months. To always seek to improve and stay ahead by at least a little ensures that your skills are always ready.

Key Takeaways:

- The web development landscape is constantly evolving, so it's important to stay up-to-date with the latest trends and technologies.
- Hotwire and Turbo are transforming the way we build Rails applications.
- API-first development, serverless computing, PWAs, and WebAssembly are all important trends to watch.
- Embrace a growth mindset and be willing to learn new things.

By embracing change and committing to lifelong learning, you'll be well-prepared to navigate the future of Rails and web development and build innovative and impactful applications.

Appendix

Think of this appendix as your handy rescue kit, filled with tools and knowledge to get you out of sticky situations and keep your Rails journey smooth. Having a cheat sheet or a reference available for each subject is great to help remember details of where everything is and how it operates!

A.1 Troubleshooting Common Errors: Debugging Demystified

Encountering errors is an inevitable part of the development process. The key is to learn how to approach these errors systematically and to know where to look for clues. As you go through the course, you will most likely face these problems sooner or later!

Here are some common Rails errors and troubleshooting tips:

1. **"NameError: uninitialized constant..."**
   o **What it means:** You're trying to use a class or module that hasn't been defined or loaded.
   o **Possible Causes:**
     ▪ Typos in class or module names.
     ▪ Missing require statements
     ▪ Incorrect file paths.
   o **Troubleshooting Steps:**
     ▪ Double-check the spelling of the class or module name.
     ▪ Ensure that the file containing the class or module is loaded (e.g., using require_relative).
     ▪ Verify that the file is located in the correct directory.
2. **"ActionView::Template::Error: undefined method ... for nil:NilClass"**
   o **What it means:** You're trying to call a method on a nil object in your view.
   o **Possible Causes:**
     ▪ The instance variable is not being set in the controller.
     ▪ The instance variable is being set to nil unexpectedly.
   o **Troubleshooting Steps:**
     ▪ Check the controller action to ensure that the instance variable is being set correctly.
     ▪ Use binding.pry or console.log to inspect the value of the instance variable at runtime.

- Verify that the object you're trying to call the method on actually exists.

3. **"ActiveRecord::RecordNotFound: Couldn't find ... with 'id'=..."**
   - **What it means:** You're trying to retrieve a record from the database that doesn't exist.
   - **Possible Causes:**
     - The ID that you're using to retrieve the record is incorrect.
     - The record has been deleted from the database.
     - The record has never been created.
   - **Troubleshooting Steps:**
     - Double-check the ID that you're using to retrieve the record.
     - Verify that the record exists in the database.
     - Handle the case where the record doesn't exist gracefully (e.g., by displaying a 404 error).

4. **"RoutingError: No route matches [HTTP verb] ..."**
   - **What it means:** The URL that you're trying to access doesn't match any of the routes defined in your config/routes.rb file.
   - **Possible Causes:**
     - Typos in the URL.
     - Missing or incorrect route definitions in config/routes.rb.
     - Incorrect HTTP verb (e.g., using GET instead of POST).
   - **Troubleshooting Steps:**
     - Double-check the URL for typos.
     - Review your config/routes.rb file to ensure that the route is defined correctly.
     - Verify that you're using the correct HTTP verb.

5. **"ActionController::RoutingError: uninitialized constant PostsController"**

- what it means: Controller name is not defined
- Most likely it involves naming convention mistakes.
- Be sure to follow the right directory and file structure to ensure Rails is able to follow.

A.2 PostgreSQL Command Reference: Quick Access to Database Power

The ability to interact directly with your PostgreSQL database is essential for troubleshooting, data analysis, and advanced data manipulation. The command to log in using postgress is

```
psql -U postgres
```

From the terminal use the code to manage the data

Basic Commands

- \l lists the databases in the system
- \c [database name] changes to a certain database
- SELECT [column] FROM [table]; outputs data of a specific table to the prompt.

A.3 Useful Rails Commands: Your Rails Cheat Sheet

Here's a cheat sheet of some of the most useful Rails commands:

- **rails new <app_name>:** Creates a new Rails application.
- **rails server:** Starts the Rails server.
- **rails console:** Opens the Rails console.
- **rails generate model <model_name>:** Generates a model and migration.
- **rails generate controller <controller_name>:** Generates a controller and views.
- **rails db:migrate:** Runs database migrations.
- **rails db:rollback:** Rolls back the last database migration.
- **rails db:seed:** Seeds the database with initial data.
- **rails routes:** Displays a list of all the routes in your application.
- **bundle install:** Installs the gems specified in your Gemfile.
- **rails test:** Runs all the tests in your application.
- **rails assets:precompile:** Precompiles your assets for production.

Key Takeaways:

- Troubleshooting errors is an essential skill for any developer.
- The official Rails documentation, Google, and other external web pages can give details to assist!
- The Rails console provides a powerful way to interact with your models and database.

This appendix serves as a handy reference for debugging problems and quickly finding the right commands, empowering you to become a more confident and efficient Rails developer. The point is to get more comfortable and find quick solutions!

www.ingramcontent.com/pod-product-compliance
Lightning Source LLC
LaVergne TN
LVHW080114070326
832902LV00015B/2575